KNITTING with PERUVIAN YARNS

KNITTING
with
PERUVIAN YARNS

25 Soft Sweaters and Accessories in Alpaca, Llama, Merino and Silk

Jane Ellison

Trafalgar Square
North Pomfret, Vermont

First published in the United States of America in 2011 by
Trafalgar Square Books,
North Pomfret,
Vermont 05053

Photographs of knitwear by Annie Bundfuss
Peruvian photographs by Glen Pearson and Peter Mulley

ISBN 978-1-57076-476-9

Library of Congress Control Number: 2010933364

10 9 8 7 6 5 4 3 2 1

Reproduction by Rival Colour Ltd, UK
Printed and bound by 1010 Printing International Ltd, China

contents

introduction

For all my knitting books, I design with the philosophy of creating simple, easy patterns with no complicated abbreviations or techniques—just straightforward patterns that let the beautiful yarns shine through. Patterns for the beginner and the experienced knitter that result in a classic handknit that should last for years to come.

My design inspiration starts with the beauty of the yarn. The designs reflect what I feel is the best use of a particular yarn. Some of the designs use a technique that slips the stitches to create a finished effect that looks similar to Fair Isle or intarsia but actually does not involve any of the complicated techniques associated with colorwork. As always, I try to create simple, and easy to follow, knitting patterns that create a unique garment, using a truly unique yarn.

When working out the designs, my first and only thought when choosing a stitch technique is: "What is easiest to knit so that the garment is a joy to knit as well as being lovely to wear?"

I love knitting and feel it is something anyone, and everyone, can do. It isn't difficult, or complicated. It is enjoyable, fun, and relaxing. Knitting is the ultimate in individuality. The beauty of the simple designs with the exciting yarns is that it results in classic garments that will last for years—as well as creating unique additions to suit any style. I hope my designs will bring joy and happiness to those who knit, or to those who receive a garment as an everlasting gift of friendship and love.

I am a creative person. I love knitting and the fact that, even if several knitters use the same pattern, each knitter will create an individual and unique garment. It is exciting that even the smallest change, like choosing a different color yarn can create something new and unique for you.

I like sharing knitting stories and techniques with other knitters. There is something lovely about sitting down together with other knitters and just chatting about different knitting styles, ideas, and techniques. With this in mind, for this book, I have included my thoughts on the design at the start of each pattern.

I hope you enjoy knitting with the high quality Mirasol yarns to make your beautiful garment and, to do so knowing that the purchase of the yarn supports such a worthwhile cause, makes it extra special.

It feels good that we can make a difference.

the Mirasol project

The Mirasol Project, named after a girl called Mirasol and all that she represents, was set up in 2006 by Michell and Company, who run the Mallkini Ranch. The company has always had the interests of its employees at heart but felt it was time to go one step further in trying to change their lives for the better.

Imagine life in the shallow air of the high Peruvian Andes, above Lake Titicaca, where the temperature can rise above 30°C (86°F) in the summer, the mountains are permanently covered in snow in winter, and the sierras are lashed with hail and biting winds. In such an environment Mirasol and her little brother Alex, help tend a flock of 350 alpaca—part of a herd of 3,000 at the Mallkini Ranch. As one of the disadvantaged Quechua-speaking people she lives with her family in a one room stone hut, without windows, or a door, and sleeps fully clothed to keep warm. Few of the Quechua people can read or write, and their health is very poor. There has been no escape from such relentless poverty. What was needed was a school.

THE MIRASOL YARN COLLECTION

Peru and the Quechua-speaking people have an ancient and rich heritage of textile artistry. The Mirasol Yarn Collection was started with the aim to raise enough money from the the sale of alpaca, wool, silk, and organic cotton yarns, from Quechua and around the world, to support the Mirasol Project. If it wasn't for the yarn made from the animals tended for generations in the Peruvian highlands, we would not have this beautiful yarn and the money to finance the building and day-to-day running of a boarding school for the children of the alpaca shepherds.

The Mirasol Yarn Collection is based on the principles of fair trade, where producers receive a price that covers sustainable production plus an extra premium that is invested in social, or economic development projects. In this way, fair trade guarantees that disadvantaged producers in the developing world get a better deal for their products. Every ball or hank bought from the Mirasol Yarn Collection contributes toward the Mirasol Project.

Although adding to the cost, the school has a boarding facility—this is vitally important because the children's families often live ten or more miles away from the ranch and attendance at the school would otherwise be impossible. The idea is for the children to stay at the school during the week and return home at weekends. So far everything has gone according to plan. Classrooms and dormitories, using local materials, have been built for the boys and girls as well as accommodation for the teaching staff and cook. There has been so much to think about: a clean water supply has been established; the kitchen equipped; linen for the beds purchased; text books and pencils chosen—even warm fleece school uniforms and pyjamas have been provided. The project is very important because currently Quechua-speaking children lag behind their contemporaries in school at all levels because the teaching is conducted in Spanish.

The aim of the Mirasol school is to make up for those differences and enable the children to reach a standard of educational excellence. One of the ways of achieving this is that here the children are being taught in both Quechua and Spanish. As well as an awareness of other cultures, there is an emphasis on the preservation of the language and customs of the children and their families. Realistic career opportunities are highlighted, and training given in local skills such as trout farming, market gardening, the breeding and care of guinea pigs, traditional textile arts, and languages. Alongside these provisions, more lofty ideals are in place where the school fosters the principles of peace, tolerance, and equality with a respect for human rights and basic freedoms. The school is a place where children can develop personal, occupational, and communication skills.

MAKING A DIFFERENCE

The school was officially opened on March 11th, 2008 to much rejoicing. The whole building was decorated with colored balloons and the classrooms were decorated with banners and drawings made by the children.

Raul Rivera for Michell and Company comments:

> "It has taken us just three years to fulfil a dream that we hardly dared believe in, but time and time again we are shown that dreams can be fulfilled. If you really want something you can move a mountain."

The school, and its ideals, has captured the imagination of many. The children are happy to entertain guests at the school, many from overseas, and are eager to learn something of their cultures. The guests bring gifts ranging from educational materials, to bicycles, and a gas

refrigerator. Stella Maris, an association of wives of the Peruvian Marine Force based at Lake Titicaca, gave each child a kit of personal items: a towel; soap; toothbrush and paste. The children were very excited by such a gift as personal hygiene items are a novelty. It seems everyone wants to help.

Jeffrey J. Denecke Jr., of Knitting Fever, the US Distributor of Mirasol Yarns, explains what involvement in the project has meant to him:

> "*Becoming a part of the Mirasol Project brought home the harsh reality of faraway places where there is a lack of even the most basic necessities such as food, shelter, drinking water, education and health care. It has also made me more conscious of how powerful a tool money can be. How even a little bit can go such a long way in helping others less fortunate, knowing the tremendous impact our efforts have had on these children.*"

Alex, Mirasol's young brother, wrote a poem to celebrate the opening of the school. Here are a few lines:

Today I have new pencils,
And little pencils of color,
What shall I draw with them?
A butterfly and a flower,
Long live the friends who help us,
Long live the Mirasol School at Mallkini!

We will leave what the children feel about their new life to 14 year-old Wilian Chunga:

> "*I come from my house to the Mirasol Boarding House. I feel good here. I learn many things and study and do my homework. The teachers are very nice. I eat food with vitamins and proteins in order to grow strong and healthy and be able to be the first. This is why I love the Mirasol Boarding House. I never dreamed of living in a house that seemed God's house because I learn many things I didn't know before. This encourages me to go on with my studies. I appreciate this with all my heart. I also thank the persons who made this possible. I send them a big hug and wish them all happiness.*
> *Thank you!*"

the Mirasol yarns used in this book

A couple of years ago, I was lucky to be able to visit the remote area that inspired the Mirasol Project. This journey made me really appreciate how much we take for granted and allowed me to experience the stunning scenery and ever changing climate of the region first hand. The light changed constantly from early morning sunrises to brilliant sunshine often mixed with rain or even hail. The distinct nature of the light and the changing weather, combine to create this climate and are mirrored in the Mirasol yarns. Each one produces a completely different look and feel—yet they all work well as a collection together.

For results that look like the projects featured in this book, always use the Mirasol yarn specified in the knitting pattern. The Mirasol Yarn Collection is constantly seeking new and exciting yarns, but sadly, they can only invest in a limited number each year. This means that yarn and shades may not be available when you come to knit a project from this book. The following yarn descriptions have been compiled to help you find a substitute yarn. It is wise to try and match the gauge as closely as possible and check the yardage of any substitute yarn. Checking the yardage will enable you to calculate the quantity of substitute yarn required. And, it is not unknown for yarn or shades to be reintroduced at a later date.

MIRASOL MISKI

Quechua meaning: fertile valley of Qhochapampa, conquered by Inka Ruka.
There aren't any words to describe Miski—and do it justice. It is the finest baby llama yarn that there ever has been (I might be very, very biased!). At first glance, the colors seem straightforward: navy, orange, or lilac.

However, a closer inspection reveals that the shades are made up of three or four different colors creating a bejewelled appearance.
Content: 100% Baby Llama. **Yardage/Weight:** 82yd/50g. **Gauge:** 4.5 sts = 1in on US 8. **Knitting Weight:** Worsted (CYCA Medium #4) yarn.

MIRASOL AKAPANA

Quechua meaning: clouds, coloring of the sky at dawn or dusk.
Akapana is a deliciously, soft yarn inspired by tweeds—yet softened with baby llama. It is made up of two strands of varying thickness, plied together. It is composed of baby llama, Merino wool, and Donegal—in natural or multicolor kneps.
Content: 65% Baby Llama, 25% Merino Wool, 10% Donegal. **Yardage/Weight:** 95yd/50g. **Gauge:** 5 sts = 1in on US 7. **Knitting Weight:** Worsted (CYCA Medium #4) yarn.

MIRASOL K'ACHA

Quechua meaning: messenger.
The beautiful combination of fibers create a luxiurious yarn that knits smoothly onto the needles. The K'acha is a roving yarn, hand

painted in tone-to-tone colors composed of fine Merino wool, suri alpaca, and silk.
Content: 60% Fine Merino Wool, 25% Alpaca, 15% Silk. **Yardage/Weight:** 98yd/50g. **Gauge:** 5.25 sts = 1in on US 6. **Knitting Weight:** DK (CYCA Light #3) yarn.

MIRASOL QINA

Quechua meaning: reed pipe, flute, bamboo flute.
A simple combination of fibers that creates a classic favorite that is a joy to knit.
The organic bamboo comes from China.
Content: 80% Baby Alpaca, 20% Bamboo. **Yardage/Weight:** 91yd/50g. **Gauge:** 5 sts = 1in on US 6.
Knitting Weight: Worsted (CYCA Medium #4) yarn.

MIRASOL SULKA

The silk gives the yarn a gorgeous sheen, which combined with the exquisite colors, may make this an enchanting yarn that a knitter can get addicted to. Like Miski, Sulka is a melange and each time I knit with it I see flecks or jewels of new color.
Content: 60% Merino Wool, 20% Alpaca, 20% Silk. **Yardage/Weight:** 55yd/50g. **Gauge:** 4 sts= 1in on US 10. **Knitting Weight:** Worsted (CYCA Medium #4) yarn.

MIRASOL TUPA

Quechua meaning: something noble, something worthy, something of exceptional quality.
Tupa has a twist that allows the silk to shine through.
Content: 50% Merino Wool, 50% Silk. **Yardage/Weight:** 137yd/50g. **Gauge:** 5.5 sts = 1in on US 6.
Knitting Weight: DK (CYCA Light #3) yarn.

MIRASOL HACHO

The yarn is unique in that it provides the warmth of Merino wool but has a crispness that reminds me of soft cotton. It is hand dyed to create the painted look that makes this yarn unique. Tupa is a single shade alternative for all the Hacho patterns.
Content: 100% Merino Wool. **Yardage/Weight:** 137yd/50g skein. **Gauge:** 5.5 sts = 1in on US 6.
Knitting Weight: DK (CYCA Light #3) yarn.

MIRASOL NUNA

Quechua meaning: soul, spirit, conscience.
Nuna is so luxuriously soft to knit with, almost delicate—but it has a strength. The Merino wool gives the yarn elasticity, which makes it a very forgiving yarn to knit with if your stitches are a little uneven—wool eases them into uniformity! The silk accepts the dye beautifully and gives the yarn that lovely deep shade, as well as a deep shine. The bamboo in Nuna isn't dyed and gives the yarn its individuality.
Content: 40% Merino Wool, 40% Silk, 20% Bamboo. **Yardage/Weight:** 191yd/50g. **Gauge:** 6 sts = 1in on US 5. **Knitting Weight:** DK (CYCA Light #3) yarn.

MIRASOL SAMP'A

Quechua meaning: light, soft, delicate, humble.
The Quechua meaning describes the yarn perfectly. Even though as a cotton it has strength, the way it is grown and dyed makes it a very delicate yarn. Samp'a is a 100% organic cotton that is spun in Holland. All the shades are naturally dyed.
Content: 100% Organic Cotton. **Yardage/ Weight:** 120yd/50g. **Gauge:** 5.5 sts = 1in on US 6. **Knitting Weight:** DK (CYCA Light #3) yarn.

All the dyestuffs used in production of the yarns are AZO-Free (except Samp'a which is made in Holland but is naturally dyed). All the yarns in the Mirasol Collection have Quechua names—the local dialect of the Quechua people.

reading patterns

SKILL LEVEL

I love knitting and I am always excited by the technique and actual knitting, just as much as the satisfaction of creating a unique garment. With this in mind I want other people to share my joy of knitting. My patterns are simple, straightforward, and easy to follow and result in beautiful, classic garments.

MATERIALS AND NEEDLES

These indicate what you will need to complete the garment. However, the quantities of yarn are based on average requirements and therefore are approximate. The needle size is only a recommendation, you may have to change the needle size to get the correct gauge.

MEASUREMENT AND SIZING INFORMATION

Everyone has a unique body shape. Before starting your garment, please check the "actual measurement" to make sure you are making the perfect size.

Each pattern includes a size guide, "to fit bust", and actual measurements which indicate the garment's length and width. Compare the measurements of a similar, well fitting garment in your closet, with the actual measurements stated in the pattern— choose the nearest pattern size.

ADJUSTING THE LENGTH

Ask a friend to measure your back from the top of your shoulder to your desired length or measure a favorite garment. Compare this length with the one in the pattern. Then,

work more or less rows before the Shape Armhole instruction on all the body pieces

The same principle applies to the sleeves. Once you have knitted the back and front, pin the shoulders and side seams together and put the garment shell on. Ask a friend to measure the distance from the top of the side seam to your desired sleeve length. Then, to lengthen or shorten the sleeve, find the instruction in the pattern that states "Continue in pattern without shaping until sleeve measures [given length] from cast on edge," and use your preferred measurement. Remember when making a custom fit garment that you may require more or less yarn than stated.

GAUGE

Every pattern has it's own unique gauge, represented as a number of stitches and rows counted over a 4in square of knitted fabric in a stated stitch pattern. To make a gauge square, first cast on the number of stitches stated, then cast on an extra four stitches. Work in the stitch pattern stated, until the square measures 5in. Do not bind off but cut the yarn and thread the tail through the stitches, taking the stitches off the needle as you do so.

To calculate the gauge, lay the square down flat, place pins to the side of a stitch near one side edge, and a second pin above a stitch near either the top or bottom edge. Using a tape measure or metal ruler, measure 4in across the square from each pin and mark with two more pins. Count the number of stitches and rows between the pins. If you have the stated number of

stitches and rows between the pins you have the correct gauge and can commence your chosen pattern.

If you have too many stitches, your gauge is tight. Change to a larger needle. If there are too few stitches, your gauge is loose. Change to a smaller needle. Repeat and work another square until you achieve the correct gauge.

STARTING TO KNIT

If you are comfortable with the techniques you use in knitting then please, continue to use them. Knitting is about finding your own enjoyment and comfort with the needles, but below are my suggestions:

Casting on

I use the thumb method—this gives a good, elastic edge.

Decreasing

I use the following to create the necklines and armholes.

K2tog or p2togtbl: generally, I use these decreases at the end of a row.

K2togtbl or sl1, k1, psso or p2tog: generally, I use these decreases at the beginning of a row.

I work decreases one stitch in from the edge.

Joining in a new ball

It is better to join in a new ball at the beginning of a row. Gently twist the new ball with the old ball at the start of the row. If at the end of the row, tie the two ends in a knot. The ends can be sewn into the seams at the finishing stage.

Stripes

All my stripes are worked so that the yarn not being used can be carried up the side. Remember not to pull the yarn too tightly up the side—this can distort the knitting.

Binding off

Bind off loosely and always in the stitch pattern being used.

abbreviations

Knitting has a language of its own. Instructions for making a knitted item are written with abbreviated terms, here are the ones I use in my book:

in	inch(es)
k	knit
m1	increase one stitch by knitting into the front and back of the next stitch
patt	pattern
p	purl
psso	pass slipped stitch over
rem	remaining
rep	repeat
rev	reverse
sl1	slip one stitch
sl2	slip two stitches
st(s)	stitch(es)
st st	stockinette stitch, knit 1 row, purl 1 row
tbl	through back of loop
tog	together
yo	yarn round needle or yarn over needle
yon	yarn over needle
yrn	yarn round needle

In the patterns, the instructions are given for the smallest size, with larger sizes in round brackets. Where only one figure or instruction is given this applies to all sizes. Work all directions inside square brackets the number of times stated.

1 Cardigans and Jackets

short-sleeved, cropped cardigan
page 18

three-quarter sleeve, wrap cardigan
page 24

high collar, short-sleeved cardigan
page 29

long, ribbed, v-neck cardigan
page 34

cropped, v-neck cardigan
page 39

edge-to-edge lace and cable, chunky jacket
page 44

lace-ribbed, hooded jacket
page 49

three-quarter length, cable coat
page 55

HACHO

short-sleeved, cropped cardigan

The length of this round-neck cardigan with lace panels, creates a fitted shape to complement any size.

MEASUREMENTS

To fit bust (suggested)	32–34	34–36	38–40	42–44	46–48	in
Actual measurement	36¼	39¼	42½	45½	49	in
Length	15¾	15¾	17¼	17¼	18	in
Sleeve length	2¾	2¾	3	3	3½	in

18

MATERIALS

DK (CYCA Light #3) yarn
Mirasol Hacho (100% Wool; 137yd/50g):
5 (6, 6, 7, 7) skeins #306.
(photographed in Hacho, Deep Blue Ocean)
For a single shade alternative: Mirasol Tupa,
(50% Merino Wool, 50% Silk; 137yd/50g)

8 (8, 8, 8, 9) small buttons

NEEDLES

One pair of US 6 knitting needles
One pair of US 5 knitting needles
Three stitch holders
Knitter's sewing needle or tapestry needle

GAUGE

22 stitches and 30 rows to 4in square over
stockinette stitch using US 6 needles.

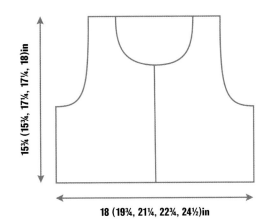

15¾ (15¾, 17¼, 17¼, 18)in

18 (19¾, 21¼, 22¾, 24½)in

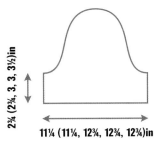

2¾ (2¾, 3, 3, 3½)in

11¼ (11¼, 12¾, 12¾, 12¾)in

Back

With US 5 needles, cast on
101 (110, 119, 128, 137) stitches.

RIB PATTERN

Row 1 (right side): K2, [p2, k3, p2, k2] to
end.
Row 2: P2, [k2, p3, k2, p2] to end.
These 2 rows form the rib pattern.
Repeat the last 2 rows until back measures
2 (2, 2¼, 2¼, 2¾)in, ending with a wrong-
side row.
Change to US 6 needles.
Starting with a purl row, work in reverse
stockinette stitch until the back measures
7 (7, 7¾, 7¾, 8¾)in from cast-on edge,
ending with a wrong-side row.

SHAPE ARMHOLES

Bind off 5 stitches at the beginning of the
next 2 rows.
(91 (100, 109, 118, 127) stitches)
Decrease one stitch at each end of the next
row and on every 4th row until 81 (90, 99,
108, 117) stitches remain.

Continue without shaping in reverse
stockinette stitch until armhole measures 8¾
(8¾, 9½, 9½, 9½)in from start of armhole
shaping, ending with a wrong-side row.

SHAPE SHOULDERS

Bind off 22 (27, 26, 31, 30) stitches at the
beginning of the next 2 rows.
Place the remaining 37 (36, 47, 46, 57)
stitches on a holder.

Left front

With US 5 needles, cast on
48 (53, 57, 62, 66) stitches.

RIB PATTERN

Row 1 (right side): K0 (3, 0, 3, 0), p0 (2, 0,
2, 0), [k2, p2, k3, p2] to last 3 stitches, k3.
Row 2: P3, [k2, p3, k2, p2] to last 0 (5, 0,
5, 0) stitches, k0 (2, 0, 2, 0), p0 (3, 0, 3, 0).

These 2 rows form the rib pattern.
Repeat the last 2 rows until left front measures 2 (2, 2¼, 2¼, 2¾)in from the cast-on edge, ending with a wrong-side row. Change to US 6 needles.

Row 1: Purl to last 31 stitches, [k1, k2tog, yo, k1, yo, k2togtbl, k1, p3] 3 times, p1.

Row 2: K1, [k3, p7] 3 times, knit to end.

Row 3: Purl to last 31 stitches, [k2tog, yo, k3, yo, k2togtbl, p3] 3 times, p1.

Row 4: Repeat row 2.

Repeat the last 4 rows until the left front measures 7 (7, 7¾, 7¾, 8¾)in from the cast-on edge, ending with a wrong-side row.

SHAPE ARMHOLE

Bind off 5 stitches at the beginning of the next row. *(43 (48, 52, 57, 61) stitches)*
Work one row.

Decrease one stitch at the armhole edge of the next row and on every 4th row until 38 (43, 47, 52, 56) stitches remain, ending with a right-side row.

SHAPE NECK

Next row: Work 11 (11, 15, 15, 19) stitches in pattern, slip these stitches on a holder, work in pattern to end.
(27 (32, 32, 37, 37) stitches)

Decrease one stitch at the neck edge of the next row and on each of the alternate rows until 22 (27, 26, 31, 30) stitches remain. Keeping pattern correct, continue without shaping until armhole measures 8¾ (8¾, 9½, 9½, 9½)in from start of armhole shaping, ending with a wrong-side row. Bind off.

Right front

With US 6 needles, cast on 48 (53, 57, 62, 66) stitches.

RIB PATTERN

Row 1 (right side): K3, [p2, k3, p2, k2] to last 0 (5, 0, 5, 0) stitches, p0 (2, 0, 2, 0), k0 (3, 0, 3, 0).

Row 2: P0 (3, 0, 3, 0), k0 (2, 0, 2, 0), [p2, k2, p3, k2] to last 3 stitches, p3.

These 2 rows form the rib pattern.
Repeat the last 2 rows until right front measures 2 (2, 2¼, 2¼, 2¾)in from the cast-on edge, ending with a wrong-side row. Change to US 6 needles.

Row 1: P1, [p3, k1, k2tog, yo, k1, yo, k2togtbl, k1] 3 times, purl to end.

Row 2: Knit to last 31 stitches, [p7, k3] 3 times, k1.

Row 3: P1, [p3, k2tog, yo, k3, yo, k2togtbl] 3 times, purl to end.

Row 4: Repeat row 2.

Repeat the last 4 rows until the right front measures 7 (7, 7¾, 7¾, 8¾)in from the cast-on edge, ending with a right-side row. Work as given for Left front, reversing armhole and neck shapings.

Sleeves

With US 5 needles, cast on 63 (63, 72, 72, 72) stitches.

RIB PATTERN

Row 1 (right side): [P2, k3, p2, k2] to end.

Row 2: [P2, k2, p3, k2] to end.

These 2 rows form the rib pattern.
Repeat the last 2 rows until sleeve measures 2 (2, 2¼, 2¼, 2¾)in from the cast-on edge, ending with a wrong-side row.

Starting with a purl row, work 6 rows in reverse stockinette stitch, ending with a wrong-side row.

SHAPE TOP

Bind off 5 stitches at the beginning of the next 2 rows. *(53 (53, 62, 62, 62) stitches)*

Decrease one stitch at each end of the next row and on every 4th row until 39 (39, 48, 48, 48) stitches remain.

Work one row.

Decrease one stitch at each end of the next row and on each of the alternate rows until 29 (29, 38, 38, 38) stitches remain.

Work 0 (0, 1, 1, 1) row.

Decrease one stitch at each end of the next row and on each of the alternate rows until 15 (15, 18, 18, 18) stitches remain.

Bind off 5 stitches at the beginning of the next 2 rows. *(5 (5, 8, 8, 8) stitches)*

Bind off remaining stitches.

Button band left edging

With right side facing and US 5 needles, pick up and knit 67 (67, 71, 71, 76) stitches down left front opening edge.

RIB PATTERN

Row 1: P3, [k2, p3, k2, p2] to last 1 (1, 5, 5, 1) stitch(es), k0 (0, 2, 2, 0), p1 (1, 3, 3, 1).

Row 2 (right side): K1(1, 3, 3, 1), p0 (0, 2, 2, 0), [k2, p2, k3, p2] to last 3 stitches, k3.

These 2 rows form the rib pattern.

Work 5 rows more in rib.

Bind off.

Buttonhole right edging

With right side facing and US 5 needles, pick up and knit 67 (67, 71, 71, 76) stitches up right front opening edge.

Starting with row 1 of the rib pattern given for the Button band left edging, work 3 rows in rib.

Buttonhole row (right side): K1 (1, 3, 3, 1), p0 (0, 2, 2, 0), [k2, p2, k2tog, yo, k1, p2] to last 3 stitches, k3.

Work 3 rows in rib.

Bind off.

Neck edging

Join shoulder seams.

With right side facing and US 5 needles, pick up and knit 7 stitches from edging, knit 11 (11, 15, 15, 19) stitches from holder at right front, pick up and knit 19 (20, 24, 24, 24) stitches up right front neck, knit 37 (36, 47, 46, 57) stitches from holder of the back, pick up and knit 20 (20, 24, 25, 24) stitches down left front neck, knit 11 (11, 15, 15, 19) stitches from holder at left front, pick up and knit 7 stitches from edging. *(112 (112, 139, 139, 157) stitches)*

RIB PATTERN

Row 1 (wrong side): P3, [k2, p3, k2, p2] to last stitch, p1.

Row 2: K3, [p2, k3, p2, k2] to last stitch, k1.

These 2 rows form the rib pattern.

Work 1 more row in rib.

Buttonhole row: K1, k2tog, yo, work in pattern to end.

Work 3 rows in rib.

Bind off.

Finish

Sew on sleeves, placing center of sleeves to shoulder seams.

Join the side and sleeve seams.

Weave in ends.

Position and sew buttons into place.

QINA

three-quarter sleeve, wrap cardigan

The yarn used for this cardigan helps create the beautiful draping. In contrast, the three-quarter sleeves make the cardigan feel fitted, and neat.

MEASUREMENTS

To fit bust (suggested)	32–34	36–38	40–42	42–44	46–48	in
Actual measurement	35½	39¼	43¼	47¼	51	in
Length	22½	22½	24½	24½	25¼	in
Sleeve length	9½	9½	9½	9½	9½	in

MATERIALS

Worsted (CYCA Medium #4) yarn
Mirasol Qina (80% Baby Alpaca, 20%
Bamboo; 91yd/50g):
yarn A, 10 (10, 11, 11, 12) skeins #902;
yarn B, 1 (1, 1, 1, 2) skeins #914.
(photographed in: yarn A, Golden Yellow;
yarn B, Dark Navy)

NEEDLES

One pair of US 6 knitting needles
Knitter's sewing needle or tapestry needle

GAUGE

20 stitches and 28 rows to 4in square over
stockinette stitch using US 6 needles.

Please note: No edges are picked up so
please make sure all edges are neat. Join
any new balls at the side edges.

Back

With US 6 needles and yarn B, cast on
90 (100, 110, 120, 130) stitches.
Starting with a knit row, work 5 rows in
stockinette stitch, ending with a right-side row.
Knit one row.
Change to yarn A.
Starting with a knit row, continue in stockinette
stitch and yarn A only until back measures
13¾ (13¾, 15, 15, 15¾)in from the cast-on
edge, ending with a wrong-side row.

SHAPE ARMHOLES

Bind off 4 stitches at the beginning of the
next 2 rows. *(92, 102, 112, 122) stitches)*
Decrease one stitch at each end of the
next row and on every 4th row until
74 (84, 94, 104, 114) stitches remain.

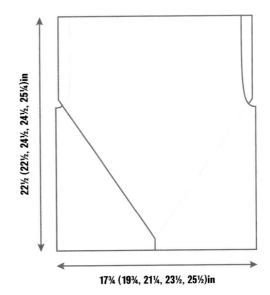

22½ (22½, 24½, 24½, 25¾)in

17¾ (19¾, 21¼, 23½, 25½)in

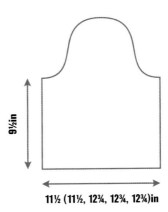

9½in

11½ (11½, 12¾, 12¾, 12¾)in

Continue without shaping in stockinette
stitch until armhole measures 8¾ (8¾, 9½,
9½, 9½)in from start of armhole shaping,
ending with a wrong-side row.

SHAPE SHOULDERS

Bind off 20 (24, 28, 32, 36) stitches at the
beginning of the next 2 rows.
Bind off the remaining 34 (36, 38, 40, 42)
stitches.

Left front

With US 6 needles and yarn B, cast on
35 (45, 55, 65, 75) stitches.

Starting with a knit row, work 5 rows in
stockinette stitch, ending with a right-side row.
Knit one row.

Change to yarn A.

Row 1 (right side): Knit to end.

Row 2: Knit to last 20 (24, 28, 32, 36)
stitches, purl to end.

These 2 rows set the position of the
stockinette stitch and garter stitch at the front
opening edge.

Keeping the stockinette stitch pattern correct
over the 20 (24, 28, 32, 36) stitches,
increase as follows, taking the increase
stitches into the garter stitch.

Increase row (right side): Knit to last
3 stitches, m1, k3.

Increase one stitch at front edge as set
above on every following alternate row, until
left front measures 13¾ (13¾, 15, 15,
15¾)in from the cast-on edge, ending with
a wrong-side row.

Continue to increase one stitch at neck edge
at the same time shape armhole as follows:

SHAPE ARMHOLE

Bind off 4 stitches at the beginning
of the next row.

Work one row.

Decrease one stitch at the armhole edge of
the next row and on every 4th row, 3 times.
Continue to increase one stitch at neck edge
as before until there are 82 (92, 102, 112,
122) stitches, ending with a right-side row.
Continue without shaping until armhole
measures 8¾ (8¾, 9½, 9½, 9½)in from
start of armhole shaping, ending with a
right-side row.

Next row: Bind off 62 (68, 74, 80, 86)
stitches, work in pattern to end.

Bind off remaining 20 (24, 28, 32, 36)
stitches.

Right front

With US 6 needles and yarn B, cast on
35 (45, 55, 65, 75) stitches.

Starting with a knit row, work 5 rows in
stockinette stitch, ending with a right-side row.
Knit one row.

Change to yarn A.

Row 1 (right side): Knit to end.

Row 2: Purl 20 (24, 28, 32, 36) stitches,
knit to end.

These 2 rows set the position of the
stockinette stitch and garter stitches at the
front opening edge.

Keeping the stockinette stitch over the
20 (24, 28, 32, 36) stitches, increase as
follows, taking the increase stitches into the
garter stitch.

Increase row (right side): K3, m1, knit to
the end.

Work as given for Left front, reversing the
shapings.

Sleeves

With US 6 needles and yarn B, cast on
59 (59, 65, 65, 65) stitches.

Starting with a knit row, work 5 rows in
stockinette stitch, ending with a right-side row.
Knit one row.

Change to yarn A.

Starting with a knit row, continue in stockinette
stitch until sleeve measures 9½in from the
cast-on edge, ending with a wrong-side row.

SHAPE TOP

Bind off 4 stitches at the beginning of the
next 2 rows.

(51 (51, 57, 57, 57) stitches)

Decrease one stitch at each end of the next
row and on every 4th row until 39 (39, 45,
45, 45) stitches remain.

Work one row.

Decrease one stitch at each end of the next
row and on each of the alternate rows until
29 (29, 35, 35, 35) stitches remain.

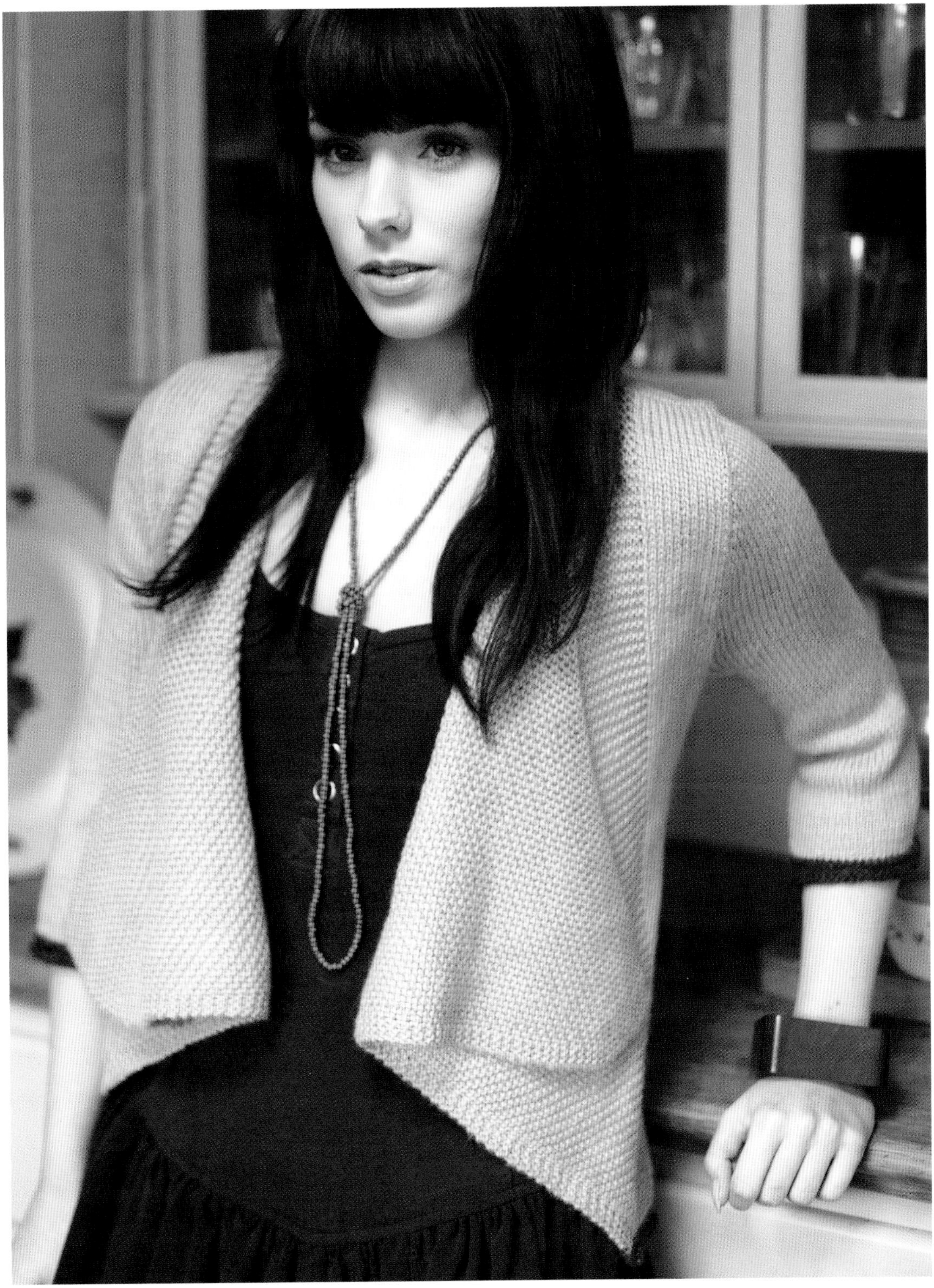

qina: three-quarter sleeve, wrap cardigan

Work 3 rows.

Decrease one stitch at each end of the next row and on every following row until 17 (17, 21, 21, 21) stitches remain.

Bind off 5 stitches at the beginning of the next 2 rows. *(7 (7, 11, 11, 11) stitches)*

Bind off remaining stitches.

Finish

Join shoulder seams.

Sew on sleeves, placing center of sleeves to shoulder seams.

Weave in ends.

Join the side and sleeve seams.

SULKA
high collar, short-sleeved cardigan

The stitches used to create this cardigan create the fitted look without any other fitted shaping. It is the subtle details that create an amazing garment and on a cardigan the buttons are particularly important. A contrasting button can create an exciting and completely different look.

MEASUREMENTS

To fit bust (suggested)	30–32	32–34	36–38	38–40	42–44	in
Actual measurement	32	35½	38¾	42¼	45½	in
Length	23½	23½	24½	26	26	in
Sleeve length	2¼	2¼	2¼	2¼	2¼	in

MATERIALS

Worsted (CYCA Medium #4) yarn
Mirasol Sulka (60% Merino Wool, 20% Alpaca, 20% Silk; 55yd/50g):
12 (12, 13, 14, 15) skeins #208.
(photographed in Paprika)

11 medium-sized buttons

NEEDLES

One pair of US 8 knitting needles
One pair of US 10 knitting needles
Five stitch holders
Knitter's sewing needle or tapestry needle

GAUGE

14 stitches and 21 rows to 4in square over stockinette stitch using US 10 needles.

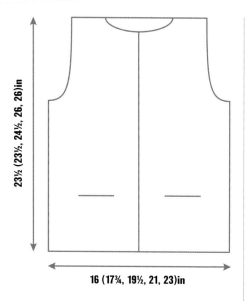

23½ (23½, 24½, 26, 26)in

16 (17¾, 19½, 21, 23)in

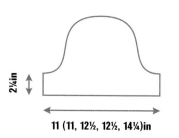

2¼in

11 (11, 12½, 12½, 14¼)in

Back

With US 10 needles, cast on
57 (63, 69, 75, 81) stitches.

RIB PATTERN

Row 1 (right side): K3, [p3, k3] to end.

Row 2: P3, [k3, p3] to end.

These 2 rows form the rib pattern.

Repeat the last 2 rows until rib measures 6in
from the cast-on edge, ending with a wrong-side row.

Starting with a knit row, continue in stockinette stitch until the back measures
15 (15, 15¾, 16½, 16½)in from the cast-on edge, ending with a wrong-side row.

SHAPE ARMHOLES

Bind off 4 stitches at the beginning of the next 2 rows. *(49 (55, 61, 67, 73) stitches)*
Decrease one stitch at each end of the next row and on every 4th row until 41 (47, 53, 59, 65) stitches remain.

Continue without shaping in stockinette stitch until armhole measures 8¾ (8¾, 8¾, 9½, 9½)in from start of armhole shaping, ending with a wrong-side row.

SHAPE SHOULDERS

Bind off 10 (12, 14, 16, 18) stitches at the beginning of the next 2 rows.

Place the remaining 21 (23, 25, 27, 29) stitches on a holder.

Pocket linings (make two)

With US 10 needles, cast on
15 (15, 15, 21, 21) stitches.

Starting with row 1 of the Back rib pattern, continue in the rib pattern until pocket lining measures 6in from the cast-on edge, ending with a wrong-side row.

Place the remaining stitches on a holder.

Left front

With US 10 needles, cast on
28 (31, 34, 37, 40) stitches.

RIB PATTERN

Row 1 (right side): P0 (3, 0, 3, 0), [k3, p3] to last 4 stitches, k4.

Row 2: P4, [k3, p3] to last 0 (3, 0, 3, 0) stitches, k0 (3, 0, 3, 0).

These 2 rows form the rib pattern.

Repeat the last 2 rows until rib measures 6in from the cast-on edge, ending with a wrong-side row.

Pocket placement row: K6 (9, 12, 9, 12) stitches, place next 15 (15, 15, 21, 21) stitches onto a holder, k15 (15, 15, 21, 21) stitches along one pocket lining, knit to end. Purl one row.

Starting with a knit row, continue in stockinette stitch until the left front measures 15 (15, 15¾, 16½, 16½)in from the cast-on edge, ending with a wrong-side row.

SHAPE ARMHOLE

Bind off 4 stitches at the beginning of the next row. *(24 (27, 30, 33, 36) stitches)*
Purl one row.

Decrease one stitch at armhole edge of the next row and on every 4th row until 20 (23, 26, 29, 32) stitches remain.

Continue without shaping in stockinette stitch until armhole measures 7 (7, 7, 7¾, 7¾)in from start of armhole shaping, ending with a right-side row.

SHAPE NECK

Next row: P6 (7, 8, 9, 10) stitches, slip these stitches on a holder, purl to end. *(14 (16, 18, 20, 22) stitches)*

Decrease one stitch at the neck edge of the next row and on every row until 10 (12, 14, 16, 18) stitches remain.

Continue without shaping in stockinette stitch until armhole measures 8¾ (8¾, 8¾, 9½, 9½)in from start of armhole shaping, ending with a wrong-side row.
Bind off.

Right front

With US 10 needles, cast on 28 (31, 34, 37, 40) stitches.

RIB PATTERN

Row 1 (right side): K4, [p3, k3] to last 0 (3, 0, 3, 0) stitches, p0 (3, 0, 3, 0).
Row 2: K0 (3, 0, 3, 0), [p3, k3] to last 4 stitches, p4.
These 2 rows form the rib pattern.
Repeat the last 2 rows until rib measures 6in from the cast-on edge, ending with a wrong-side row.

SHAPE TOP

Bind off 4 stitches at the beginning of the next 2 rows. *(31 (31, 37, 37, 43) stitches)*
Decrease one stitch at each end of the next row and on every 4th row until 21 (21, 27, 27, 33) stitches remain.
Purl one row.
Decrease one stitch at each end of the next row and on each of the alternate rows until 13 (13, 19, 19, 25) stitches remain.
Decrease one stitch at each end of the next row and on every following row until 7 (7, 9, 9, 15) stitches remain.
Bind off 3 (3, 4, 4, 7) stitches at the beginning of the next 2 rows. *(1 stitch)*
Bind off remaining stitch.

Collar

Join shoulder seams.

With right side facing and US 8 needles, knit 6 (7, 8, 9, 10) stitches from holder at right front, pick up and knit 10 (11, 9, 10, 11) stitches up right front neck, knit 21 (23, 25, 27, 29) stitches from holder for the back, pick up and knit 10 (11, 9, 10, 11) stitches along left front neck, knit 6 (7, 8, 9, 10) stitches from holder at left front.
(53 (59, 59, 65, 71) stitches)

RIB PATTERN

Row 1 (wrong side): P4, [k3, p3] to last stitch, p1.
Row 2: K4, [p3, k3] to last stitch, k1.
Repeat the last 2 rows until collar measures 4in, ending with a right-side row.
Next row (right side): K4, [p3, k3] to last stitch, k1.
Next row: P4, [k3, p3] to last stitch, p1.
Repeat the last 2 rows until collar measures 8¾in, ending with a wrong-side row.
Bind off.

Pocket placement row: K7, place next 15 (15, 15, 21, 21) stitches onto a holder, k15 (15, 15, 21, 21) stitches along one pocket lining, knit to end.
Purl one row.
Complete as given for Left front, but reversing shapings.

Sleeves

With US 10 needles, cast on 39 (39, 45, 45, 51) stitches.
Starting with row 1 of the Back rib pattern, continue in the rib pattern until sleeve measures 2in from the cast-on edge, ending with a wrong-side row.
Starting with a knit row, continue in stockinette stitch until sleeve measures 2¼in from the cast-on edge, ending with a wrong-side row.

Left edging

With right side facing and US 8 needles, measure 4¾in down from top of collar, pick up and knit 17 stitches up left collar from this point, break yarn, slip these stitches onto needle, with same needle then pick up and knit 15 stitches down left edge of collar and pick up and knit 81 (81, 84, 87, 87) stitches down left edge.
(113 (113, 116, 119, 119) stitches)

RIB PATTERN
Row 1: P4 (4, 1, 4, 4), *k3, p3, repeat from * to last 19 stitches, [p3, k3] to last stitch, k1.
Row 2: P4, [k3, p3] twice, k3, *k3, p3, repeat from * to last 4 (4, 1, 4, 4) stitches, knit to end.
Work the rib row 1 again.
Buttonhole row: P4, bind off 3 stitches, work in the pattern to end.
Next row: Work in the pattern, casting on 3 stitches over those bound off on previous row.
Work 3 more rows in rib pattern.
Bind off.

Right edging

With right side facing and US 8 needles, pick up and knit 81 (81, 84, 87, 87) stitches up right front opening edge and pick up and knit 15 stitches up right edge of collar to same point as on left edge, break yarn, with another needle then pick up and knit 17 stitches down right edge of collar, break yarn and slip these stitches onto the needle with the other stitches.
113 (113, 116, 119, 119) stitches)
Rejoin yarn with wrong-side facing.

RIB PATTERN
Row 1: K1 [k3, p3] 3 times, *p3, k3, repeat from * to last 4 (4, 1, 4, 4) stitches, p4 (4, 1, 4, 4).
Row 2: K4, (4, 1, 4, 4,), *p3, k3, repeat from * to the last 19 stitches, [k3, p3] 3 times, p1.

Work the rib row 1 again.
Buttonhole row: K4, bind off 3 stitches, [rib 9 stitches, bind off 3 stitches] 4 times, work in pattern to end.
Next row: Work in pattern to end, casting on 3 stitches over those bound off on previous row.
Work 3 more rows in rib pattern.
Bind off.

Pocket tops

With right side facing and US 10 needles, work in pattern 15 (15, 15, 21, 21) stitches from pocket top holder.

RIB PATTERN
Row 1: P3, [k3, p3] to end.
Row 2 (right side): K3, [p3, k3] to end.
Buttonhole row: Work in pattern for 6 (6, 6, 9, 9) stitches, bind off 3 stitches, work in pattern to end.
Next row: Work in pattern, casting on 3 stitches over those bound off on previous row.
Work 3 rows in rib.
Bind off.

Finish

Sew on sleeves, placing center of sleeves to shoulder seams.
Join the side and sleeve seams.
Position and sew buttons into place.
Sew pocket linings in place on wrong side.
Catch down sides of pocket tops.
Weave in ends.

QINA
long, ribbed, v-neck cardigan

A long, ribbed, v-neck cardigan is so practical and easy to wear. To make your cardigan unique, experiment with the shades to match others in your closet.

MEASUREMENTS

To fit bust (suggested)	32–34	36–38	38–40	42–44	44–46	in
Actual measurement	38	40½	43	45¼	47½	in
Length	26¾	27½	28¼	29¼	29¼	in
Sleeve length	17¾	17¾	17¾	17¾	17¾	in

MATERIALS

Worsted (CYCA Medium #4) yarn
Mirasol Qina (80% Baby Alpaca, 20%
Bamboo; 91yd/50g):
yarn A, 12 (13, 13, 14, 14) skeins #915;
yarn B, 1 (1, 1, 1, 1) skein #902;
yarn C, 1 (1, 2, 2, 2) skeins #909;
yarn D, one skein #901.
(photographed in: yarn A, Slate Grey; yarn B,
Golden Yellow; yarn C, Charcoal Black;
yarn D, Steel)

3 snaps

NEEDLES

One long US 5 circular needle
One pair of US 5 knitting needles
One pair of US 6 knitting needles
Four stitch holders
Knitter's sewing needle or tapestry needle

GAUGE

20 stitches and 28 rows to 4in square over
main pattern using US 6 needles.

Back

With US 6 needles with yarn B, cast on
97 (103, 109, 115, 121) stitches.

RIB PATTERN

Row 1 (right side): Knit to end.
Change to yarn C.
Row 2: P1, [p2, k1] to last 3 stitches, p3.
These 2 rows form the rib stitch pattern.
Work a further 4 rows in the rib stitch in yarn
C only.
Change to yarn D.
Repeat rib row 1.
Working with yarn A only:

MAIN PATTERN

Row 1 (wrong side): P3, k1, [p5, k1] to
last 3 stitches, p3.
Row 2 (right side): Knit to end.
These 2 rows form the main stitch pattern.

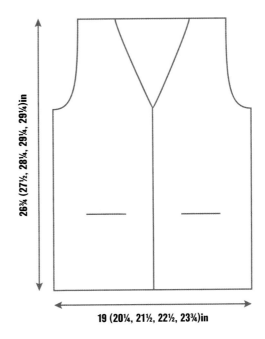

26¾ (27½, 28¼, 29¼, 29¼)in

19 (20¼, 21½, 22½, 23¾)in

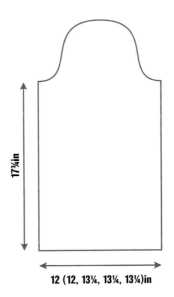

17¾in

12 (12, 13¼, 13¼, 13¼)in

Repeat the last 2 rows until back measures 18 (18¾, 18¾, 19¾, 19¾)in from the cast-on edge, ending with a wrong-side row.

SHAPE ARMHOLES
Bind off 5 stitches at the beginning of the next 2 rows.
(87 (93, 99, 105, 111) stitches)
Decrease one stitch at each end of the next row and on every 4th row until 77 (83, 89, 95, 101) stitches remain.
Continue without shaping in the main stitch pattern until armhole measures 8¾ (8¾, 9½, 9½, 9½)in from start of armhole shaping, ending with a wrong-side row.

SHAPE SHOULDERS
Bind off 21 (23, 25, 27, 29) stitches at the beginning of next 2 rows.
Place the remaining 35 (37, 39, 41, 43) stitches on a holder.

Pocket linings (make two)
With US 6 needles and yarn A, cast on 25 (25, 31, 31, 37) stitches.
Starting with row 2 of the main stitch pattern as given for the Back, work as given for the Back until pocket lining measures 6 (6½, 6½, 7½, 7½)in from the cast-on edge, ending with a wrong-side row.
Place the stitches on a holder.

Left front
With US 6 needles and yarn B, cast on 46 (49, 52, 55, 58) stitches.

RIB PATTERN
Row 1 (right side): Knit to end.
Change to yarn C.
Row 2: P1, [p2, k1] to last 3 stitches, p3.
These 2 rows form the rib stitch pattern.
Work a further 4 rows in the rib stitch in yarn C only.
Change to yarn D.
Repeat rib row 1.

Working with yarn A only:

MAIN STITCH PATTERN
Row 1 (wrong side): P0 (3, 0, 3, 0), k1, [p5, k1] to last 3 stitches, p3.
Row 2 (right side): Knit to end.
These 2 rows form the main stitch pattern.
Repeat the last 2 rows until left front measures 7 (7¾, 7¾, 8¾, 8¾)in from the cast-on edge, ending with a wrong-side row.
Pocket placement row: Knit 12 stitches, place next 25 (25, 31, 31, 37) stitches onto a holder, knit 25 (25, 31, 31, 37) stitches along one pocket lining, knit to end.
Continue in main stitch pattern until left front measures 18 (18¾, 18¾, 19¾, 19¾)in from the cast-on edge, ending with a wrong-side row.

SHAPE ARMHOLE AND NECK
Bind off 5 stitches at the beginning of the next row. *(41 (44, 47, 50, 53) stitches)*
Work one row.
Decrease one stitch at the armhole edge on the next row and on every 4th row, at the same time decrease one stitch at the neck edge on the next row and on every 2 (4, 3, 5, 7) alternate rows and then, on every following 4th row until 21 (23, 25, 28, 29) stitches remain.
Continue without shaping in main stitch pattern until armhole measures 8¾ (8¾, 9½, 9½, 9½)in from start of armhole shaping, ending with a wrong-side row.
Bind off.

Right front

With US 6 needles and yarn B, cast on
46 (49, 52, 55, 58) stitches.

RIB PATTERN

Row 1 (right side): Knit to end.

Change to yarn C.

Row 2: P1, [p2, k1] to last 3 stitches, p3.
These 2 rows form the rib stitch pattern.

Work a further 4 rows in the rib stitch in yarn
C only.

Change to yarn D.

Repeat rib row 1.

Working with yarn A only:

MAIN PATTERN

Row 1 (wrong side): P3, [k1, p5] to last
1 (4, 1, 4, 1) stitches, k1, p0 (3, 0, 3, 0).

Row 2 (right side): Knit to end.

Repeat the last 2 rows until right front
measures 7 (7¾, 7¾, 8¾, 8¾)in from the
cast-on edge, ending with a wrong-side row.

Pocket placement row: Knit 9 (12, 9, 12, 9)
stitches, place the next 25 (25, 31, 31, 37)
stitches onto a holder, knit 25 (25, 31, 31,
37) stitches along one pocket lining, knit to
the end.

Continue in main stitch pattern until right
front measures 18 (18¾, 18¾, 19¾, 9¾)in
from the cast-on edge, ending with a right-
side row.

Work as given for Left front, reversing shape
armhole and neck.

Sleeves

With US 6 needles and yarn B, cast on 61 (61, 67, 67, 67) stitches.

Work as given for the back until sleeve measures 17¾in from the cast-on edge, ending with a wrong-side row.

SHAPE TOP

Bind off 5 stitches at the beginning of the next 2 rows. *(51 (51, 57, 57, 57) stitches)*

Decrease one stitch at each end of the next row and on every 4th row until 35 (35, 41, 41, 41) stitches remain.

Work one row.

Decrease one stitch at each end of the next row and on each of the alternate rows until 21 (21, 27, 27, 27) stitches remain.

Work one row.

Decrease one stitch at each end of the next row and on every following row until 9 (9, 11, 11, 11) stitches remain.

Bind off remaining stitches.

Pocket tops

With right side facing, US 5 needles and yarn D, pick up and knit 25 (25, 31, 31, 37) stitches from pocket top holder.

With yarn C, work 5 rows in main pattern.

With yarn B, knit one row.

Bind off in pattern with yarn B on the wrong-side row.

Edging

Join shoulder seams.

With right side facing, using a long US 5 circular needle and yarn B, pick up and knit 2 stitches, with yarn C, pick up and knit 4 stitches, with yarn D, pick up and knit one stitch, with yarn A pick up and knit 120 (123, 127, 129, 129) stitches up right front opening edge, knit 35 (37, 39, 41, 43) stitches from holder at back neck, pick up and knit 120 (124, 127, 129, 130) stitches down left front opening edge, with yarn D pick up and knit one stitch, with yarn C pick up and knit 4 stitches, with yarn B pick up and knit 2 stitches. *(289 (298, 307, 313, 316) stitches)*

Row 1 (wrong side): With yarn B, p2, with yarn C, p1, k1, p2, with yarn D, k1, with yarn A, p2 [p2, k1] to last 9 stitches, with yarn D, k1, with yarn C, p2, k1, p1, with yarn B, p2.

Row 2: With yarn B, k2, with yarn C, k4, with yarn D, k1, with yarn A, knit to last 7 stitches, with yarn D, k1, with yarn C, k4, with yarn B, k2.

Repeat row 1 once more.

Row 4: With yarn B, k2, with yarn C, k4, with yarn D, knit until the last 6 stitches, with yarn C, k4, with yarn B, k2.

Row 5: With yarn B, p2, with yarn C, p1, k1, [p2, k1] to last 3 stitches, with yarn C, p1, with yarn B, p2.

Row 6: With yarn B, k2, with yarn C, knit until the last 2 stitches, with yarn B, k2.

Repeat the last 2 rows once more.

Repeat row 5 again.

Row 10: With yarn B, p1, [p2, k1] to last 3 stitches, p3.

With yarn B, bind off knitwise.

Finish

Sew on sleeves, placing center of sleeves to shoulder seams.

Join the side and sleeve seams.

Position and sew snaps into place.

Sew pocket linings in place on wrong side.

Catch down sides of pocket tops.

Weave in ends.

TUPA
cropped, v-neck cardigan

This cardigan plays with one of my favorite techniques—the slip stitch. This technique creates a fabric that looks complicated but is actually really easy to do—the best type of knitting! Even, subtle shade changes can transform the whole look of the cardigan.

MEASUREMENTS

To fit bust (suggested)	32–34	34–36	36–38	40–42	42–44	in
Actual measurement	35½	37¼	39¼	42¾	46¼	in
Length	17¼	17¼	19	19¾	20½	in
Sleeve length	8¾	8¾	8¾	9½	9½	in

MATERIALS

DK (CYCA Light #3) yarn
Mirasol Tupa (50% Merino Wool, 50% Silk; 137yd/50g):
yarn A, 3 (3, 4, 4, 5) skeins #809;
yarn B, 5 (6, 6, 7, 7) skeins #804.
(photographed in: yarn A, Sapphire;
yarn B, Viridian)

3 small buttons

NEEDLES

One long US 5 circular knitting needle
One pair of US 5 knitting needles
One pair of US 6 knitting needles
One stitch holder
Knitter's sewing needle or tapestry needle

GAUGE

26 stitches and 48 rows to 4in square over pattern using US 6 needles.

Note: When slipping the stitch on a wrong-side row bring the yarn forward so that it is on the wrong side when slipping, then take it back to knit the next stitch.

Back

With US 5 needles and yarn B, cast on 350 (368, 392, 422, 458) stitches.

EDGING FRILL

Decrease row 1 (right side): [K2tog] to end.
(175 (184, 196, 211, 229) stitches)
Decrease row 2: P1, [p2tog, p1] to end.
(117 (123, 131, 141, 153) stitches)

RIB PATTERN

Row 1: K1, [p1, k1] to end.
Row 2: P1, [k1, p1] to end.
These 2 rows form the rib pattern.
Repeat the last 2 rows until back measures 4in from the cast-on edge, ending with a wrong-side row.
Change to US 6 needles.

SLIP STITCH PATTERN

Row 1: With yarn A, k1, [sl1, k1] to end.
Row 2: With yarn A, sl1, [k1, sl1] to end.
Row 3: With yarn B, repeat row 1.
Row 4: With yarn B, repeat row 2.
These 4 rows form the slip stitch pattern.
Repeat the last 4 rows until back measures 8¾ (8¾, 9½, 10¼, 11)in from the cast-on edge, ending with a wrong-side row.

SHAPE ARMHOLES

Bind off 5 stitches at the beginning of the next 2 rows.
(107 (113, 121, 131, 143) stitches)
Decrease one stitch at each end of the next row and on every 4th row until 97 (103, 111, 121, 133) stitches remain.
Continue without shaping in pattern until armhole measures 8¾ (8¾, 9½, 9½, 9½)in

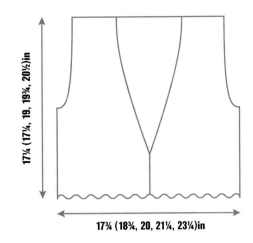

17¼ (17¼, 19, 19¾, 20½)in

17¾ (18¾, 20, 21¼, 23¼)in

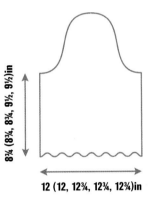

8¾ (8¾, 8¾, 9½, 9½)in

12 (12, 12¾, 12¾, 12¾)in

from start of armhole shaping, ending with a wrong-side row.

SHAPE SHOULDERS

Bind off 27 (29, 33, 37, 41) stitches at the beginning of the next 2 rows.
Place the remaining 43 (45, 45, 47, 51) stitches on a holder.

Left front

With US 5 needles and yarn B, cast on
176 (182, 194, 212, 230) stitches.

EDGING FRILL

Decrease row 1 (right side): [K2tog] to end.
(88 (91, 97, 106, 115) stitches)

Decrease row 2: P1, [p2tog, p1] to end.
(59 (61, 65, 71, 77) stitches)

Starting with rib row 1 of the Back, work in
the rib pattern until left front measures 4in
from the cast-on edge, ending with a wrong-
side row.

Change to US 6 needles.

Starting with slip stitch pattern row 1 of the
Back, work 4 rows in the slip stitch pattern.
Continue to work slip stitch pattern and work
neck shaping as follows:

SHAPE NECK

Next row: Work in pattern to last 5 stitches,
k2tog, work 3 stitches in pattern.

Work 3 rows in pattern.

Keeping pattern correct, decrease one stitch
as set at neck edge on the next row and on
every 4th row until left front measures 8¾
(8¾, 9½, 10¼, 11)in from the cast-on
edge, ending with a wrong-side row and 3
rows straight since last decrease.

SHAPE ARMHOLE AND NECK

Next row: Bind off 5 stitches, work in the
pattern to last 5 stitches, k2tog, work
3 stitches in pattern.

Work one row in pattern.

Decrease one stitch at the armhole edge on
the next row and 4 more times on every 4th
row, at the same time continue to decrease
one stitch at neck edge on every 4th row
until 27 (29, 33, 37, 41) stitches remain.
Continue without shaping in pattern until
armhole measures 8¾ (8¾, 9½, 9½, 9½)in
from start of armhole shaping, ending with a
wrong-side row.

Bind off.

Right front

With US 5 needles, cast on
176 (182, 194, 212, 230) stitches.

Starting with edging frill decrease row 1, work
as given for the Left front until shape neck.

SHAPE NECK

Next row: K3, s1 knitwise, k1, psso, pattern
to end.

Work as for Left front, reversing shapings.

Sleeves

With US 5 needles and yarn B, cast on
236 (236, 254, 254, 254) stitches.

EDGING FRILL

Decrease row 1 (right side): [K2tog] to end.
(118 (118, 127, 127, 127) stitches)

Decrease row 2: P1, [p2tog, p1] to end.
(79 (79, 85, 85, 85) stitches)

Starting with rib row 1 of the Back, work in
the rib pattern until left front measures 2in
from the cast-on edge, ending with a wrong-
side row.

Change to US 6 needles.

Starting with slip stitch pattern row 1 of the
Back, work until sleeve measures 8¾ (8¾,
8¾, 9½, 9½)in from the cast-on edge,
ending with a wrong-side row.

SHAPE TOP

Bind off 5 stitches at the beginning of the
next 2 rows.

(69 (69, 75, 75, 75) stitches)

Decrease one stitch at each end of the next
row and on every 4th row until 51 (51, 57,
57, 57) stitches remain.

Work one row in pattern.

Decrease one stitch at each end of the next
row and on each of the alternate rows until
39 (39, 45, 45, 45) stitches remain.

Work one row in pattern.

Decrease one stitch at each end of the next
row and on every following row until 15
(15, 19, 19, 19) stitches remain.

Bind off.

Neck edging

Join shoulder seams.

With right side facing, yarn B and long circular US 5 needle, pick up and knit 90 (90, 95, 100, 105) stitches up right front edging from top of frill, knit 43 (45, 45, 47, 51) stitches from holder at center back, pick up and knit 90 (90, 95, 100, 105) stitches down left front edging to top of frill.
(223 (225, 235, 247, 261) stitches)
Next row: Knit to last 16 stitches, k2tog, yo, [k4, yo, k2tog] to last 2 stitches, k2.
Knit one row.
Bind off on wrong-side row.

Finish

Sew on sleeves, placing center of sleeves to shoulder seams.
Join the side and sleeve seams.
Position and sew buttons into place.
Weave in ends.

SULKA

edge-to-edge lace and cable, chunky jacket

This jacket plays with traditional ideas and uses a solid chunky yarn to create a delicate lace pattern, next to a structured cable pattern. In contrast, the rolled edgings let the fabric do what it does naturally.

MEASUREMENTS

To fit bust (suggested)	32–36	38–42	44–52	in
Actual measurement	36¼	46½	57¼	in
Length	24½	26¼	28½	in
Sleeve length	15¾	15¾	16½	in

MATERIALS

Worsted (CYCA Medium #4) yarn
Mirasol Sulka (60% Merino Wool, 20% Alpaca, 20% Silk; 55yd/50g): 18 (20, 22) skeins #221. (photographed in Denim Blue)

One decorative clasp

NEEDLES

One pair of US 8 knitting needles
One pair of US 10 knitting needles
One cable needle
Three stitch holders
Knitter's sewing needle or tapestry needle

GAUGE

15 stitches and 18 rows to 4in square over lace pattern using US 10 needles.

SPECIAL ABBREVIATIONS

C2B: Slip next stitch onto cable needle and hold at back, k1 from left-hand needle, k1 from cable needle.

C4B: Slip next 2 stitches onto cable needle and hold at back, k2 from left-hand needle, k2 from cable needle.

C4F: Slip next 2 stitches onto cable needle and hold at front, k2 from left-hand needle, k2 from cable needle.

T2B: Slip next stitch onto cable needle and hold at back, k1 from left-hand needle, p1 from cable needle.

T2F: Slip next stitch onto cable needle and hold at front, p1 from left-hand needle, k1 from cable needle.

T4B: Slip next 2 stitches onto cable needle and hold at back, k2 from left-hand needle, p2 from cable needle.

T4F: Slip next 2 stitches onto cable needle and hold at front, p2 from left-hand needle, k2 from cable needle.

Back and fronts

These are knitted in one piece up to armholes.
With US 10 needles, cast on 159 (199, 239) stitches.
Knit 2 rows.

MAIN STITCH PATTERN

Row 1 (right side): K2, p4, T4F, p1, C2B, p1, T4B, p4, k3, [yo, k3, sl1, k2tog, psso, k3, yo, k1] to last 24 stitches, k2, p4, T4F, p1, C2B, p1, T4B, p4, k2.

Row 2: P2, k6, [p2, k1] twice, p2, k6, p2, purl to last 24 stitches, p2, k6, [p2, k1] twice, p2, k6, p2.

Row 3: T4F, p4, T4F, T4B, p4, T4B, p1, [k1, yo, k2, sl1, k2tog, psso, k2, yo, k1, p1] to last 24 stitches, T4F, p4, T4F, T4B, p4, T4B.

Row 4: K2, p2, k6, p4, k6, p2, k3, [p9, k1] to last 24 stitches, k2, p2, k6, p4, k6, p2, k2.

Row 5: P2, C4F, p4, T2F, T2B, p4, C4B, p3, [k2, yo, k1, sl1, k2tog, psso, k1, yo, k2, p1] to last 24 stitches, p2, C4F, p4, T2F, T2B, p4, C4B, p2.

Row 6: K2, p4, k5, p2, k5, p4, k3, [p9, k1] to last 24 stitches, k2, p4, k5, p2, k5, p4, k2.

Row 7: T4B, T4F, p3, C2B, p3, T4B, T4F, p1, [k3, yo, sl1, k2tog, psso, yo, k3, p1] to last 24 stitches, T4B, T4F, p3, C2B, p3, T4B, T4F.

Row 8: P2, k4, [p2, k3] twice, p2, k4, p2, purl to last 24 stitches, p2, k4, [p2, k3] twice, p2, k4, p2.

These 8 rows form the main stitch pattern. Repeat the last 8 rows until work measures 16½ (17½, 17¾)in from the cast-on edge, ending with a wrong-side row.
Divide for fronts.

RIGHT FRONT

Next row: Work in pattern until there are 45 (55, 65) stitches on right hand needle, turn, place the remaining stitches on a holder.

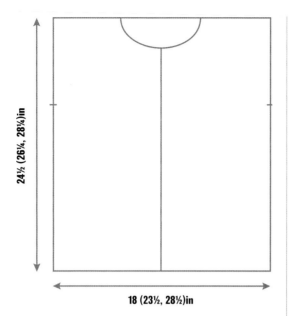

24½ (26¼, 28¼)in

18 (23½, 28½)in

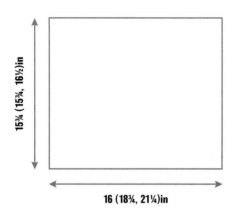

15¾ (15¾, 16½)in

16 (18¾, 21¼)in

Keeping pattern correct, continue to work on these 45 (55, 65) stitches until work measures 21¼ (23¼, 25)in from the cast-on edge, ending with a wrong-side row.

SHAPE NECK

Next row: Work 11 (16, 21) stitches in pattern, place these 11 (16, 21) stitches on a holder, work in pattern to end.
(34 (39, 44) stitches)
Work one row in pattern.
Decrease one stitch at neck edge on the next row and on every following row until 24 (29, 34) stitches remain.
Continue in pattern without shaping until work measures 24½ (26¼, 28¼)in from the cast-on edge, ending with a wrong-side row.
Bind off.

BACK

With right side facing, rejoin yarn to center 69 (89, 109) stitches, increasing one stitch at each end of row. *(71 (91, 111) stitches)*
Keeping pattern correct with first and last stitch as knit on right side and purl on wrong side, continue in pattern until work measures 24½ (26¼, 28¼)in from the cast-on edge, ending with a wrong-side row.

SHAPE SHOULDERS

Bind off 24 (29, 34) stitches at the beginning of the next 2 rows.
Place remaining 23 (33, 43) stitches on a holder.

LEFT FRONT

Rejoin yarn to remaining 45 (55, 65) stitches, work in pattern to end.
Work as for Right front, reversing shapings.

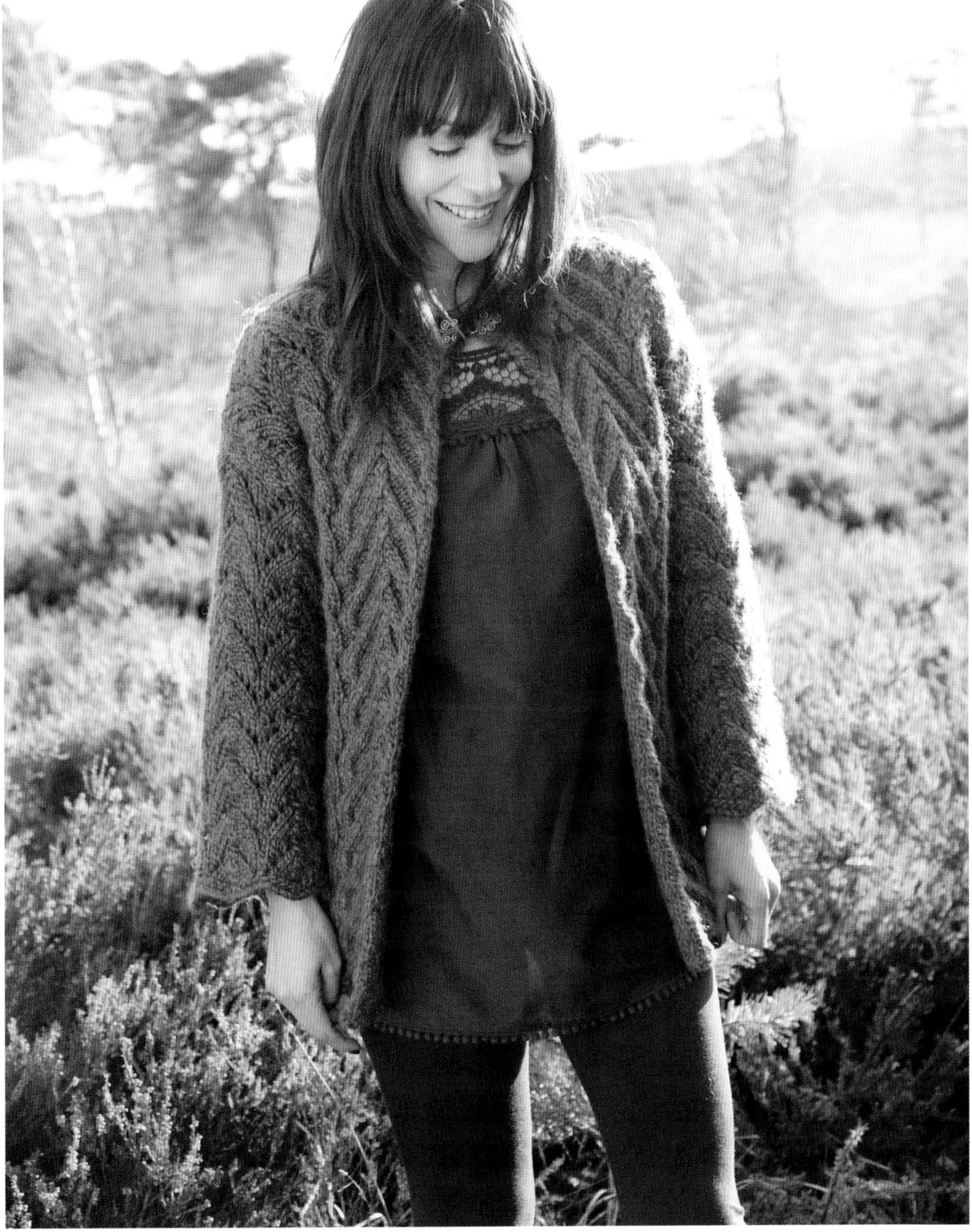

sulka: edge-to-edge lace and cable, chunky jacket

Sleeves

With US 10 needles, cast on
61 (71, 81) stitches.
Knit 2 rows.

MAIN STITCH PATTERN

Row 1 (right side): K1, [yo, k3, sl1, k2tog, psso, k3, yo, k1] to end.

Row 2: Purl to end.

Row 3: P1, [k1, yo, k2, sl1, k2tog, psso, k2, yo, k1, p1] to end.

Row 4: K1, [p9, k1] to end.

Row 5: P1, [k2, yo, k1, sl1, k2tog, psso, k1, yo, k2, p1] to end.

Row 6: Repeat row 4.

Row 7: P1, [k3, yo, sl1, k2tog, psso, yo, k3, p1] to end.

Row 8: Purl to end.

These 8 rows form the pattern.

Repeat the last 8 rows until sleeve measures 15¾ (15¾, 16½)in from the cast-on edge, ending with a wrong-side row.

Bind off.

Neck edge

Join shoulder seams.

With right side facing and US 8 needles, knit 11 (16, 21) stitches from holder at right front, pick up and knit 9 stitches up right front neck, knit 23 (33, 43) stitches from holder at back, pick up and knit 9 stitches down left front neck, knit 11 (16, 21) stitches from holder at left front.

(63 (83, 103) stitches)

Knit one row.

Bind off.

Finish

Sew on sleeves, placing center of sleeves to shoulder seams.

Join the sleeve seams. Weave in ends.

Attach decorative clasp to fasten neck edge as shown in photograph on page 47.

SAMP'A
lace-ribbed, hooded jacket

The lace in this jacket makes it light to wear, while the ribbing and the slight shaping give the garment a flattering fitted look. The partnering of the lace with the hood means this jacket looks just as good with either a floral dress or t-shirt and jeans.

MEASUREMENTS

To fit bust (suggested)	30–32	32–34	36–38	38–40	42–44	in
Actual measurement	33	36½	39¾	43	46¼	in
Length	26½	26½	26¾	27½	28¼	in
Sleeve length	10¼	10¼	10¼	10¼	10¼	in

MATERIALS

DK (CYCA Light #3) yarn
Mirasol Samp'a (100% Organic Cotton; 120yd/50g):
13 (14, 15, 16, 17) skeins #604.
(photographed in Berry Red)

Open ended zipper to fit

NEEDLES

One long circular US 3 knitting needle
One pair of US 5 knitting needles
Three stitch holders
Knitter's sewing needle or tapestry needle

GAUGE

24 stitches and 30 rows to 4in square over pattern using US 5 needles.

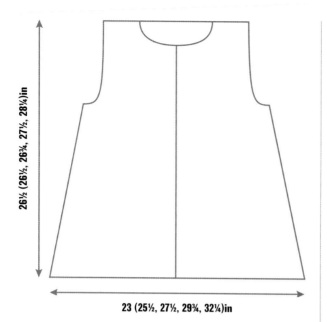

26½ (26½, 26¾, 27½, 28¼)in

23 (25½, 27½, 29¾, 32¼)in

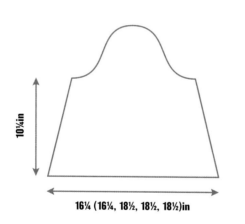

10¼in

16¼ (16¼, 18½, 18½, 18½)in

Back

With US 5 needles, cast on
141 (155, 169, 183, 197) stitches.

CABLE LACE PATTERN

Rows 1, 3, and 5 (wrong side): P2, k4,
[p3, k4] to last 2 stitches, p2.

Row 2 (right side): K2, p4, [yo, sl1, k2tog,
psso, yo, p4, k3, p4] to last 9 stitches, yo,
sl1, k2tog, psso, yo, p4, k2.

Row 4: K2, p4, [k1, yo, sl1, k1, psso, p4,
k3, p4] to last 9 stitches, k1, yo, sl1, k1,
psso, p4, k2.

Row 6: K2, p4, [k3, p4] to last 2 stitches, k2.
These last 6 rows form the cable lace pattern.
Repeat the last 6 rows until the back
measures 7¾ (7¾, 8¼, 8¾, 9½)in from
the cast-on edge, ending with row 6 of the
cable lace pattern repeat.

Decrease row (wrong side): P2, k2, k2tog,
[p3, k2, k2tog] to last 2 stitches, p2.
(121 (133, 145, 157, 169) stitches)

Row 1 (right side): K2, p3, [yo, sl1, k2tog,
psso, yo, p3, k3, p3] to last 8 stitches, yo,
sl1, k2tog, psso, yo, p3, k2.

Rows 2, 4, and 6 (wrong side): P2, k3,
[p3, k3] to last 2 stitches, p2.

Row 3: K2, P3, [k1, yo, sl1, k1, psso, p3,
k3, p3] to last 8 stitches, k1, yo, sl1, k1,
psso, p3, k2.

Row 5: K2, P3, [k3, p3] to last 2 stitches, k2.
These last 6 rows form the pattern.
Repeat the last 6 rows until the back
measures 13¾ (13¾, 14¼, 15, 15¾)in
from the cast-on edge, ending with row 5 of
the pattern repeat.

Decrease row (wrong side): P2, k1, k2tog,
[p3, k1, k2tog] to last 2 stitches, p2.
(101 (111, 121, 131, 141) stitches)

Row 1 (right side): K2, p2, [yo, sl1, k2tog,
psso, yo, p2, k3, p2] to last 7 stitches, yo,
sl1, k2tog, psso, yo, p2, k2.

Rows 2, 4, and 6 (wrong side): P2, k2,
[p3, k2] to last 2 stitches, p2.

Row 3: K2, p2, [k1, yo, sl1, k1, psso, p2,

k3, p2] to last 7 stitches, k1, yo, sl1, k1, psso, p2, k2.

Row 5: K2, p2, [k3, p2] to last 2 stitches, k2.

These last 6 rows form the pattern.

Repeat the last 6 rows until back measures 17¾ (17¾, 18, 18, 18¾)in from the cast-on edge, ending with a wrong-side row.

SHAPE ARMHOLES

Bind off 5 stitches at the beginning of the next 2 rows.

(91 (101, 111, 121, 131) stitches)

Decrease one stitch at each end of the next row and on every 4th row until 79 (89, 99, 109, 119) stitches remain.

Keeping pattern correct, continue without shaping until armhole measures 8¾ (8¾, 8¾, 9½, 9½)in from start of armhole shaping, ending with a wrong-side row.

SHAPE SHOULDERS

Bind off 19 (22, 26, 30, 34) stitches at the beginning of the next 2 rows. Place 41 (45, 47, 49, 51) stitches on a holder.

Left front

With US 5 needles, cast on 72 (79, 86, 93, 100) stitches.

CABLE LACE PATTERN

Rows 1, 3, and 5 (wrong side): [P3, k4] to last 2 stitches, p2.

Row 2 (right side): K2, p0 (4, 0, 4, 0), k0 (3, 0, 3, 0), [p4, yo, sl1, k2tog, psso, yo, p4, k3] to end.

Row 4: K2, p0 (4, 0, 4, 0), k0 (3, 0, 3, 0), [p4, k1, yo, sl1, k1, psso, p4, k3] to end.

Row 6: K2, [p4, k3] to end.

These last 6 rows form the cable lace pattern.

Repeat the last 6 rows until the left front measures 7¾ (7¾, 8¼, 8¾, 9½)in from the cast-on edge, ending with row 6 of the cable lace pattern repeat.

Decrease row (wrong side): [P3, k2, k2tog] to last 2 stitches, p2.

(62 (68, 74, 80, 86) stitches)

Row 1 (right side): K2, p0 (2, 0, 2, 0), k0 (3, 0, 3, 0), [p2, yo, sl1, k2tog, psso, yo, p2, k3] to end.

Rows 2, 4, and 6 (wrong side): [P3, k2] to last 2 stitches, p2.

Row 3: K2, p0 (2, 0, 2, 0), k0 (3, 0, 3, 0), [p2, k1, yo, sl1, k1, psso, p2, k3] to end.

Row 5: K2, [p2, k3] to end.

These last 6 rows form the pattern.

Repeat the last 6 rows until left front measures 17¾ (17¾, 18, 18, 18¾)in from the cast-on edge, ending with a wrong-side row.

SHAPE ARMHOLE

Bind off 5 stitches at the beginning of the next row. *(47 (52, 57, 62, 67) stitches)*

Work one row in pattern.

Decrease one stitch at armhole edge of the next row and on every 4th row until 41 (46, 51, 56, 61) stitches remain.

Continue without shaping in pattern until armhole measures 6¼ (6¼, 6¼, 7, 7)in from start of armhole shaping, ending with a right-side row.

SHAPE NECK

Next row (wrong side): Work 16 (18, 19, 20, 21) stitches in pattern, slip these stitches onto a holder, work in pattern to end. *(25 (28, 32, 36, 40) stitches)*

Decrease one stitch at the neck edge of the next row and on each of the alternate rows until 19 (22, 26, 30, 34) stitches remain.

Continue without shaping in pattern until armhole measures 8¾ (8¾, 8¾, 9½, 9½)in from start of armhole shaping, ending with a wrong-side row.

Bind off.

Row 1 (right side): K2, p0 (3, 0, 3, 0), k0 (3, 0, 3, 0), [p3, yo, sl1, k2tog, psso, yo, p3, k3] to end.

Rows 2, 4, and 6 (wrong side): [P3, k3] to last 2 stitches, p2.

Row 3: K2, p0 (3, 0, 3, 0), k0 (3, 0, 3, 0), [p3, k1, yo, sl1, k1, psso, p3, k3] to end.

Row 5: K2, [p3, k3] to end.

These last 6 rows form the pattern.

Repeat the last 6 rows until the left front measures 13¾ (13¾, 14¼, 15, 15¾)in from the cast-on edge, ending with row 5 the pattern repeat.

Decrease row (wrong side): [P3, k1, k2tog] to last 2 stitches, p2.
(52 (57, 62, 67, 72) stitches)

Right front

With US 5 needles, cast on
72 (79, 86, 93, 100) stitches.

CABLE LACE PATTERN

Rows 1, 3, and 5 (wrong side): P2, [k4, p3]
to end.

Row 2 (right side): [K3, p4, yo, sl1, k2tog,
psso, yo, p4] to last 2 (9, 2, 9, 2) stitches,
k0 (3, 0, 3, 0), p0 (4, 0, 4, 0), k2.

Row 4: [K3, p4, k1, yo, sl1, k1, psso, p4]
to last 2 (9, 2, 9, 2) stitches, k0 (3, 0, 3, 0),
p0 (4, 0, 4, 0), k2.

Row 6: [K3, p4] to last 2 stitches, k2.
These last 6 rows form the cable lace pattern.
Repeat the last 6 rows until the right front
measures 7¾ (7¾, 8¼, 8¾, 9½)in from
the cast-on edge, ending with row 6 of the
cable lace pattern repeat.

Decrease row (wrong side): P2, [k2, k2tog,
p3] to end. *(62 (68, 74, 80, 86) stitches)*

Row 1 (right side): [K3, p3, yo, sl1, k2tog,
psso, yo, p3] to last 2 (8, 2, 8, 2) stitches,
k0 (3, 0, 3, 0), p0 (3, 0, 3, 0), k2.

Rows 2, 4, and 6 (wrong side): P2, [k3, p3]
to end.

Row 3: [K3, p3, k1, yo, sl1, k1, psso, p3]
to last 2 (8, 2, 8, 2) stitches, k0 (3, 0, 3, 0),
p0 (3, 0, 3, 0), k2.

Row 5: [K3, p3] to last 2 stitches, k2.
These last 6 rows form the pattern.
Repeat the last 6 rows until the right front
measures 13¾ (13¾, 14¼, 15, 15¾)in
from the cast-on edge, ending with row 5 of
the pattern repeat.

Decrease row (wrong side): P2, [k1,k2tog,
p3] to end.
(52 (57, 62, 67, 72) stitches)

Row 1 (right side): [K3, p2, yo, sl1, k2tog,
psso, yo, p2] to last 2 (7, 2, 7, 2) stitches,
k0 (3, 0, 3, 0), p0 (2, 0, 2, 0), k2.

Rows 2, 4, and 6 (wrong side): P2, [k2, p3]
to end.

Row 3: [K3, p2, k1, yo, sl1, k1, psso, p2]
to last 2 (7, 2, 7, 2) stitches, k0 (3, 0, 3,
0), p0 (2, 0, 2, 0), k2.

Row 5: [K3, p2] to last 2 stitches, k2.
These last 6 rows form the pattern.
Work as given for Left front, reversing
armhole and neck shapings.

Sleeves

With US 5 needles, cast on
99 (99, 113, 113, 113) stitches.

CABLE AND LACE PATTERN

Rows 1, 3, and 5 (wrong side): P2, k4,
[p3, k4] to last 2 stitches, p2.

Row 2 (right side): K2, p4, [yo, sl1, k2tog,
psso, yo, p4, k3, p4] to last 9 stitches, yo,
sl1, k2tog, psso, yo, p4, k2.

Row 4: K2, p4, [k1, yo, sl1, k1, psso, p4,
k3, p4] to last 9 stitches, k1, yo, sl1, k1,
psso, p4, k2.

Row 6: K2, p4, [k3, p4] to last 2 stitches, k2.
These last 6 rows form the cable lace pattern.
Repeat the last 6 rows until the sleeve
measures 3½in from the cast-on edge,
ending with row 6 of the cable lace pattern.

Decrease row (wrong side): P2, k2, k2tog,
[p3, k2, k2tog] to last 2 stitches, p2.
(85 (85, 97, 97, 97) stitches)

Row 1 (right side): K2, p3, [yo, sl1, k2tog,
psso, yo, p3, k3, p3] to last 8 stitches, yo,
sl1, k2tog, psso, yo, p3, k2.

Rows, 2, 4, and 5 (wrong side): P2, k3,
[p3, k3] to last 2 stitches, p2.

Row 3: K2, p3, [k1, yo, sl1, k1, psso, p3,
k3, p3] to last 8 stitches, k1, yo, sl1, k1,
psso, p3, k2.

Row 5: K2, p3, [k3, p3] to last 2 stitches, k2.
These last 6 rows form the pattern.
Repeat the last 6 rows until the sleeve
measures 7in from the cast-on edge, ending
with row 5 of the pattern.

Decrease row (wrong side): P2, k1, k2tog, [p3, k1, k2tog] to last 2 stitches, p2.
(71 (71, 81, 81, 81) stitches)
Row 1 (right side): K2, p2, [yo, sl1, k2tog, psso, yo, p2, k3, p2] to last 7 stitches, yo, sl1, k2tog, psso, yo, p2, k2.
Rows, 2, 4, and 5 (wrong side): P2, k2, [p3, k2] to last 2 stitches, p2.
Row 3: K2, p2, [k1, yo, sl1, k1, psso, p2, k3, p2] to last 7 stitches, k1, yo, sl1, k1, psso, p2, k2.
Row 5: K2, p2, [k3, p2] to last 2 stitches, k2.
These last 6 rows form the pattern.
Repeat the last 6 rows until sleeve measures 10¼in from the cast-on edge, ending with a wrong-side row.

SHAPE TOP

Bind off 5 stitches at the beginning of the next 2 rows. *(61 (61, 71, 71, 71) stitches)*
Decrease one stitch at each end of the next row and on every 4th row 47 (47, 57, 57, 57) stitches remain.
Work one row in pattern.
Decrease one stitch at each end of the next row and on each of the alternate rows until 35 (35, 45, 45, 45) stitches remain.
Work one row in pattern.
Decrease one stitch at each end of the next row and on every following row until 15 (15, 21, 21, 21) stitches remaining.
Bind off 5 stitches at the beginning of the next 2 rows. *(5 (5, 11, 11, 11) stitches)*
Bind off remaining stitches.

Hood

Join shoulder seams.
With right side facing and US 5 needles, knit 16 (18, 19, 20, 21) stitches from holder at right front, pick up and knit 13 (14, 14, 12, 13) stitches up right front neck, knit 41 (45, 47, 49, 51) stitches from holder at center back, pick up and knit 12 (13, 14, 12, 12) stitches down left front neck, knit 16 (18, 19, 20, 21) stitches from holder at left front.

(98 (108, 113, 113, 118) stitches)
Row 1: P3, [k2, p3] to end.
Row 2: K3, [p2, k3] to end.
Repeat the last 2 rows until hood measures 13¾in ending with a wrong-side row.
Bind off.

Edging

Join bound off edges of hood.
With right side facing and using a long circular US 3 needle, pick up and knit 116 (116, 119, 122, 125) stitches up right front opening edge, pick up and knit 74 stitches along right side of hood edging, pick up and knit 74 stitches down left side of hood and pick up and knit 116 (116, 119, 122, 125) stitches down left front opening edge.
(380 (380, 386, 392, 398) stitches)
Knit one row.
Bind off.

Finish

Sew on sleeves, placing center of sleeves to shoulder seams.
Join the side and sleeve seams.
Position and sew zipper into place.
Weave in ends.

MISKI
three-quarter length, cable coat

The cable stitch pattern of this coat creates a beautiful texture and fitted look and it falls gently over your hips and thighs.

MEASUREMENTS

To fit bust (suggested)	32–34	36–38	38–40	42–44	46–48	in
Actual measurement	36½	40	43¼	46½	49¾	in
Length	27½	27½	28¼	28¼	28¼	in
Sleeve length	17¾	17¾	17¾	17¾	17¾	in

MATERIALS

Worsted (CYCA Medium #4) yarn
Mirasol Miski (100% Baby Llama; 82yd/50g):
yarn A, 16 (16, 17, 17, 18) skeins #117;
yarn B, 1 (1, 1, 1, 1) skein #106.
(photographed in: yarn A, Mississippi; yarn B, French Navy)

8 large buttons

NEEDLES

One pair of US 6 knitting needles
One pair of US 8 knitting needles
Cable needle
Three stitch holders
Knitter's sewing needle or tapestry needle

GAUGE

24 stitches and 24 rows to 4in square over pattern when slightly stretched using US 8 needles.

SPECIAL ABBREVIATIONS

C4B: Slip next 2 stitches onto cable needle and hold at back, k2 from left-hand needle, k2 from cable needle.

C4F: Slip next 2 stitches onto cable needle and hold at front, k2 from left-hand needle, k2 from cable needle.

Back

With US 8 needles and yarn B, cast on 154 (168, 182, 196, 210) stitches. Change to yarn A.

CABLE PATTERN

Row 1 (right side): P3, [k8, p6] to last 11 stitches, k8, p3.

Rows 2 and 4: K3, [p8, k6] to last 11 stitches, p8, k3.

Row 3: P3, [C4B, C4F, p6] to last 11 stitches, C4B, C4F, p3.

These 4 rows form the cable pattern.

Repeat the last 4 rows until back measures 7in from the cast-on edge, ending with row 3 of the repeat.

Decrease row (wrong side): K1, k2tog, [p8, k2togtbl, k2, k2tog] to last 11 stitches, p8, k2togtbl, k1.

(132 (144, 156, 168, 180) stitches)

Row 1: P2, [k8, p4] to last 10 stitches, k8, p2.

Rows 2 and 4: K2, [p8, k4] to last 10 stitches, p8, k2.

Row 3: P2, [C4B, C4F, p4] to last 10 stitches, C4B, C4F, p2.

These 4 rows form the pattern.

Repeat the last 4 rows until back measures 13¼in from the cast-on edge, ending with row 3 of the repeat.

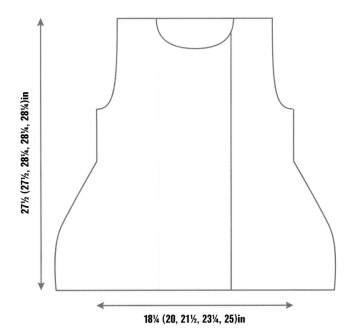

27½ (27½, 28¼, 28¼, 28¼)in

18¼ (20, 21½, 23¼, 25)in

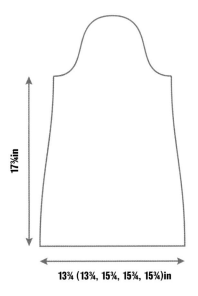

17¾in

13¾ (13¾, 15¾, 15¾, 15¾)in

Decrease row (wrong side): K2, [p8, k2togtbl, k2tog] to last 10 stitches, p8, k2. *(112 (122, 132, 142, 152) stitches)*

Row 1: P2, [k8, p2] to end.

Rows 2 and 4: K2, [p8, k2] to end.

Row 3: P2, [C4B, C4F, p2] to end.

These 4 rows form the pattern.

Repeat the last 4 rows until back measures 18¾in from the cast-on edge, ending with a wrong-side row.

SHAPE ARMHOLES

Bind off 5 stitches at the beginning of the next 2 rows.

(102 (112, 122, 132, 142) stitches)

Decrease one stitch at each end of the next row and on every 4th row until 92 (102, 112, 122, 132) stitches remain.

Continue without shaping in pattern until armhole measures 8¾ (8¾, 9½, 9½, 9½)in from start of armhole, ending with a wrong-side row.

SHAPE SHOULDERS

Bind off 23 (27, 30, 34, 39) stitches at the beginning of the next 2 rows.

Next row: K5 (3, 0, 6, 1), k2 (0, 0, 0, 0) tog, p2, [k2togtbl, k4, k2tog, p2] to last 7 (3, 0, 6, 1) stitches, k2 (0, 0, 0, 0) togtbl, k5 (3, 0, 6, 1).

Place 38 (40, 42, 46, 44) stitches on a stitch holder.

Left front

With US 8 needles and yarn B, cast on 89 (95, 103, 109, 117) stitches.

Change to yarn A.

CABLE PATTERN

Row 1 (right side): P3, *k8, p6, repeat from * to last 30 (36, 30, 36, 30) stitches, [k4, p2] 5 (6, 5, 6, 5) times.

Rows 2 and 4: [K2, p4] 5 (6, 5, 6, 5) times, *k6, p8, repeat from * to last 3 stitches, k3.

Row 3: P3, *C4B, C4F, p6, repeat from * to last 30 (36, 30, 36, 30) stitches, [k4, p2]

5 (6, 5, 6, 5) times.

These 4 rows form the cable pattern.

Repeat the last 4 rows until left front measures 7in from the cast-on edge, ending with row 3 of the repeat.

Decrease row (wrong side): [K2, p4] 5 (6, 5, 6, 5) times, *k2togtbl, k2, k2tog, p8, repeat from * to last 3 stitches, k2togtbl, k1. *(80 (86, 92, 98, 104) stitches)*

Row 1: P2, *k8, p4, repeat from * to last 30 (36, 30, 36, 30) stitches, [k4, p2] 5 (6, 5, 6, 5) times.

Rows 2 and 4: [K2, p4] 5 (6, 5, 6, 5) times, *k4, p8, repeat from * to last 2 stitches, k2.

Row 3: P2, *C4B, C4F, p4, repeat from * to last 30 (36, 30, 36, 30) stitches, [k4, p2] 5 (6, 5, 6, 5) times.

These 4 rows form the pattern. Repeat the last 4 rows until left front measures 13¼in from the cast-on edge, ending with row 3 of the repeat.

Decrease row (wrong side): [K2, p4] 5 (6, 5, 6, 5) times, *k2togtbl, k2tog, p8, repeat from * to last 2 stitches, k2. *(72 (78, 82, 88, 92) stitches)*

Row 1: P2, *k8, p2, repeat from * to last 30 (36, 30, 36, 30) stitches, [k4, p2] 5 (6, 5, 6, 5) times.

Rows 2 and 4: [K2, p4] 5 (6, 5, 6, 5) times, *k2, p8, repeat from * to last 2 stitches, k2.

Row 3: P2, *C4B, C4F, p2, repeat from * to last 30 (36, 30, 36, 30) stitches, [k4, p2] 5 (6, 5, 6, 5) times.

These 4 rows form the pattern.

Repeat the last 4 rows until left front measures 18¾in from the cast-on edge, ending with a wrong-side row.

SHAPE ARMHOLE

Bind off 5 stitches at the beginning of the next row. *(67 (73, 77, 83, 87) stitches)*

Work one row in pattern.

Decrease one stitch at armhole edge of the next row and on every 4th row until 62 (68, 72, 78, 82) stitches remain.

Continue without shaping in pattern until armhole measures 5½ (5½, 6¼, 6¼, 6¼)in from start of armhole shaping, ending with a right-side row.

SHAPE NECK

Next row: Work 32 (36, 36, 36, 36) stitches in pattern, place these stitches on a holder, work in pattern to end.

(30 (32, 36, 42, 46) stitches)

Decrease one stitch at neck edge of the next row and on each of the alternate rows until 23 (27, 30, 34, 39) stitches remain.

Continue without shaping in pattern until armhole measures 8¾ (8¾, 9½, 9½, 9½)in from start of armhole shaping ending with a wrong-side row.

Bind off.

Mark positions for 3 buttons along front opening edge, first one 17in from the cast-on edge, second one ½in from the bound-off edge, and remaining button placed evenly between the two.

Right front

With US 8 needles and yarn B, cast on 89 (95, 103, 109, 117) stitches.

Change to yarn A.

CABLE PATTERN

Row 1 (right side): [P2, k4] 5 (6, 5, 6, 5) times, *p6, k8, repeat from * to last 3 stitches, p3.

Rows 2 and 4: K3, *p8, k6, repeat from * to last 30 (36, 30, 36, 30) stitches, [p4, k2] 5 (6, 5, 6, 5) times.

Row 3: [P2, k4] 5 (6, 5, 6, 5) times, *p6, C4B, C4F, repeat from * to last 3 stitches, p3.

These 4 rows form the cable pattern.

Repeat the last 4 rows until right front measures 7in from the cast-on edge, ending with row 3 of the repeat.

Decrease row (wrong side): K1, k2tog, *p8, k2togtbl, k2, k2tog, repeat from * to last 30 (36, 30, 36, 30) stitches, [p4, k2] 5 (6, 5, 6, 5) times.

(80 (86, 92, 98, 104) stitches)

Row 1: [P2, k4] 5 (6, 5, 6, 5) times, *p4, k8, repeat from * to last 2 stitches, p2.

Rows 2 and 4: K2, *p8, k4, repeat from * to last 30 (36, 30, 36, 30) stitches, [p4, k2] 5 (6, 5, 6, 5) times.

Row 3: [P2, k4] 5 (6, 5, 6, 5) times, *p4, C4B, C4F, repeat from * to last 2 stitches, p2.

These 4 rows form the pattern. Repeat the last 4 rows until right front measures 13¼in from the cast-on edge, ending with row 3 of the repeat.

Decrease row (wrong side): K2, *p8, k2togtbl, k2tog, repeat from * to last 30 (36, 30, 36, 30) stitches, [p4, k2] 5 (6, 5, 6, 5) times.

(72 (78, 82, 88, 92) stitches)

Row 1: [P2, k4] 5 (6, 5, 6, 5) times, *p2, k8, repeat from * to last 2 stitches, p2.

Rows 2 and 4: K2, *p8, k2, repeat from * to last 30 (36, 30, 36, 30) stitches, [p4, k2] 5 (6, 5, 6, 5) times.

Row 3: [P2, k4] 5 (6, 5, 6, 5) times, *p2, C4B, C4F, repeat from * to last 2 stitches, p2.

These 4 rows form the pattern.

Work as given for the Left front, reversing shaping and working buttonholes as below to correspond with positions marked on left front.

Buttonhole row 1 (right side): P2, k1, bind off 2 stitches (1 stitch on right needle after cast off), p2, [k4, p2] twice, k1, bind off 2 stitches, work in pattern to end.

Buttonhole row 2 (wrong side): Work in pattern to end, casting on 2 stitches over those bound off on previous row.

Sleeves

With US 8 needles and yarn B, cast on 84 (84, 96, 96, 96) stitches.

Change to yarn A.

CABLE PATTERN

Row 1 (right side): P2, [k8, p4] to last 10 stitches, k8, p2.

Rows 2 and 4: K2, [p8, k4] to last 10 stitches, p8, k2.

Row 3: P2, [C4B, C4F, p4] to last 10 stitches, C4B, C4F, p2.

These 4 rows form the cable pattern.

Repeat the last 4 rows until sleeve measures 4in from the cast-on edge, ending with row 3 of the repeat.

Decrease row (wrong side): K2, [p8, k2togtbl, k2tog] to last 10 stitches, p8, k2. *(72 (72, 82, 82, 82) stitches)*

Row 1: P2, [k8, p2] to end.

Rows 2 and 4: K2, [p8, k2] to end.

Row 3: P2, [C4B, C4F, p2] to end.

These 4 rows form the pattern.

Repeat the last 4 rows until sleeve measures 17¾in from the cast-on edge, ending with a wrong-side row.

SHAPE TOP

Bind off 5 stitches at the beginning of the next 2 rows.

(62 (62, 72, 72, 72) stitches)

Decrease one stitch at each end of the next row and on every 4th row until 50 (50, 60, 60, 60) stitches remain.

Work 3 rows in pattern.

Decrease one stitch at each end of the next row and on each of the alternate rows until 40 (40, 50, 50, 50) stitches remain.

Work one row in pattern.

Decrease one stitch at each end of the next row and on every following row until 18 (18, 20, 20, 20) stitches remain.

Bind off 5 stitches at the beginning of the next 2 rows. *(8 (8, 10, 10, 10) stitches)*

Bind off remaining stitches.

Collar

Join shoulder seams.

With right side facing, US 6 needles and yarn A, rib 32 (36, 36, 36, 36) stitches from holder at right front, pick up and knit 16 (13, 16, 18, 15) stitches up right front neck, rib 38 (40, 42, 46, 44) stitches from holder at the back, pick up and knit 16 (13, 16, 18, 15) stitches down left front neck, rib 32 (36, 36, 36, 36) stitches from holder at left front. *(134 (138, 146, 154, 146) stitches)*

RIB PATTERN

Row 1 (wrong side): [K2, p4] 5 (6, 6, 6, 6) times, *k2, p6, repeat from * to last 32 (38, 38, 38, 38) stitches, k2, [p4, k2] to end.

Row 2: [P2, k4] 5 (6, 6, 6, 6) times, *p2, k6, repeat from * to last 32 (38, 38, 38, 38) stitches, p2, [k4, p2] to end.

These 2 rows form the rib pattern.

Repeat the last 2 rows until collar measures 3¼in, ending with a wrong-side row.

Work the buttonhole rows 1 and 2 as given for the right front.

Work in rib pattern until collar measures 4¾in, ending with a right-side row.

Change to yarn B.

Work one row in rib.

Bind off with yarn B.

Finish

Sew on sleeves, placing center of sleeves to shoulder seams.

Join the side and sleeve seams.

Position and sew buttons into place.

Weave in ends.

2 Sweaters

**textured
stripe,
loose-fitting
sweater**
page 64

**zig zag,
high-collared
sweater**
page 68

**sweater with
elongated
neck-opening**
page 72

**sloppy-joe
inspired,
raglan
sweater**
page 77

**wide-neck
sweater with
ruffly stripes**
page 81

K'ACHA

textured stripe, loose-fitting sweater

This sweater plays with a basic rib. One row is replaced with a knit row and another with lace, to create this loose-fitting garment.

MEASUREMENTS

To fit bust (suggested)	32–34	36–38	38–40	42–44	46–48	in
Actual measurement	40	41¾	45	48	51	in
Length	24½	24½	30	30	30	in
Sleeve length	18	18	18	18	18	in

64

MATERIALS

DK (CYCA Light #3) yarn
Mirasol K'acha (60% Fine Merino Wool,
25% Alpaca, 15% Silk; 98yd/50g):
yarn A, 12 (13, 13, 14, 14) skeins #1200;
yarn B, one skein #1205.
(photographed in: yarn A, Trinity Cream;
yarn B, Dark Chocolate)

NEEDLES

One pair of US 6 knitting needles
Knitter's sewing needle or tapestry needle

GAUGE

20 stitches and 30 rows to 4in square over
garter stitch rib pattern using US 6 needles.

Back and front alike

With US 6 needles and yarn B, cast on
102 (106, 114, 122, 130) stitches.
Change to yarn A.

LACE PATTERN

Row 1 (right side): K1, *k2tog, [yo] twice,
sl1, k1, psso, repeat from * to last stitch, k1.
Row 2: P1, *p1, [k1, p1] into double yo, p1,
repeat from * to last stitch, p1.
These 2 rows form the lace rib pattern.
Repeat the last 2 rows a further 8 times.

GARTER STITCH RIB PATTERN

Row 1: Knit to end.
Row 2: P2, [k2, p2] to end.
These 2 rows form the garter stitch rib pattern.
Repeat the last 2 rows a further 8 times.
The last 36 rows form the pattern repeat.
Repeat the last 36 rows a further 3 (3, 4, 4,
4) times.

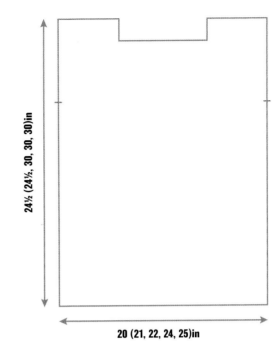

24½ (24½, 30, 30, 30)in

20 (21, 22, 24, 25)in

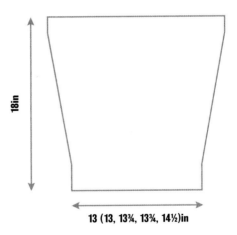

18in

13 (13, 13¾, 13¾, 14½)in

SHAPE ONE NECK AND SHOULDER
Next row: Work 28 (30, 33, 37, 40) stitches in pattern, turn and place remaining 74 (76, 81, 85, 90) stitches on a holder.
Work in garter stitch rib pattern on these 28 (30, 33, 37, 40) stitches until the work measures 2in.
Bind off.

SHAPE THE OTHER NECK AND SHOULDER
With right side facing, bind off center 46 (46, 48, 48, 50) stitches purlwise, work in pattern to end.
Work to match one neck and shoulder.

Sleeves
With US 6 needles and yarn B, cast on 66 (66, 70, 70, 74) stitches.
Change to yarn A.
Starting with row 1 of the Back and front alike lace pattern, continue in the pattern until sleeve measures 2in from the cast-on edge, ending with a wrong-side row.
Keeping pattern correct, increase one stitch at each end of next and every following 6th row until there are 86 (86, 90, 90, 94) stitches.
Continue without shaping in pattern until sleeve measures 18in from the cast-on edge, ending with a wrong-side row.
Bind off.

Finish
Join shoulder seams.
Sew on sleeves, placing center of sleeves to shoulder seams.
Join the side and sleeve seams.
Weave in ends.

k'acha: textured stripe, loose-fitting sweater

SULKA
zig zag, high-collared sweater

The zig zag or chevron is a favorite motif of mine. Worked in a soft yarn with a sheen, this sweater uses stitches to create a subtle zig zag.

MEASUREMENTS

To fit bust (suggested)	32–34	36–38	38–40	42–44	46–48	in
Actual measurement	35¾	39¾	43¾	47½	51½	in
Length	26½	26½	28¼	28¼	29	in
Sleeve length	17¾	17¾	17¾	17¾	17¾	in

MATERIALS
Worsted (CYCA Medium #4) yarn
Mirasol Sulka (60% Merino Wool, 20% Alpaca, 20% Silk; 55yd/50g):
yarn A, 23 (23, 24, 24, 25) skeins #222;
yarns B, one skein #202.
(photographed in: yarn A, Red Onion; yarn B, Lime)

NEEDLES
One pair of US 8 knitting needles
One pair of US 10 knitting needles
Two stitch holders
Knitter's sewing needle or tapestry needle

GAUGE
16 stitches and 24 rows to 4in square over chevron pattern using US 10 needles.

Back and front alike
With US 10 needles and yarn B, cast on 73 (81, 89, 97, 105) stitches.
Change to yarn A.

CHEVRON PATTERN
Row 1 (right side): K1, [p7, k1] to end.
Row 2: P1, [k7, p1] to end.
Row 3: K2, [p5, k3] to last 7 stitches, p5, k2.
Row 4: P2, [k5, p3] to last 7 stitches, k5, p2.
Row 5: K3, [p3, k5] to last 6 stitches, p3, k3.
Row 6: P3, [k3, p5] to last 6 stitches, k3, p3.
Row 7: K4, [p1, k7] to last 5 stitches, p1, k4.
Row 8: P4, [k1, p7] to last 5 stitches, k1, p4.
Row 9: Repeat row 2.
Row 10: Repeat row 1.
Row 11: Repeat row 4.
Row 12: Repeat row 3.
Row 13: Repeat row 6.
Row 14: Repeat row 5.
Row 15: Repeat row 8.
Row 16: Repeat row 7.
These 16 rows form the chevron pattern.

Repeat the last 16 rows until work measures 17¾ (17¾, 18¾, 18¾, 19½)in from the cast-on edge, ending with a wrong-side row.

SHAPE ARMHOLES

Bind off 4 stitches at the beginning of the next 2 rows. *(65 (73, 81, 89, 97) stitches)*
Decrease one stitch at each end of the next row and on every 4th row until 57 (65, 73, 81, 89) stitches remain.
Continue without shaping in chevron pattern until armhole measures 5½ (5½, 6¼, 6¼, 6¼)in from start of armhole shaping, ending with a wrong-side row.

SHAPE LEFT NECK

Next row: Work in pattern until there are 20 (24, 27, 30, 34) stitches on right-hand needle, place remaining stitches on a stitch holder, turn.
Work one row in pattern.
Decrease one stitch at the neck edge of the next row and on each of the alternate rows until 14 (18, 21, 24, 28) stitches remain.
Continue without shaping in chevron pattern until armhole measures 8¾ (8¾, 9½, 9½, 9½)in from start of armhole shaping, ending with a wrong-side row.
Bind off.

SHAPE RIGHT NECK

With right side facing, leave center 17 (17, 19, 21, 21) stitches on a stitch holder, rejoin yarn to remaining 20 (24, 27, 30, 34) stitches, work in pattern to end.
Work to match left neck, reversing shapings.

69

Sleeves

With US 10 needles and yarn B, cast on 57 (57, 65, 65, 65) stitches.

Change to yarn A.

Starting with row 1 of the chevron pattern as given for the Back and front alike, continue in the chevron pattern until sleeve measures 17¾in from the cast-on edge, ending with a wrong-side row.

SHAPE TOP

Bind off 4 stitches at the beginning of the next 2 rows.

(49 (49, 57, 57, 57) stitches)

Decrease one stitch at each end of the next row and on every 4th row until 37 (37, 45, 45, 45) stitches remain.

Work one row in pattern.

Decrease one stitch at each end of the next row and on each of the alternate rows until 27 (27, 35, 35, 35) stitches remain.

Work one row in pattern.

Decrease one stitch at each end of the next row and on each following row until 9 (9, 11, 11, 11) stitches remain.

Bind off 3 (3, 4, 4, 4) stitches at the beginning of the next 2 rows. *(3 stitches)*

Bind off remaining stitches.

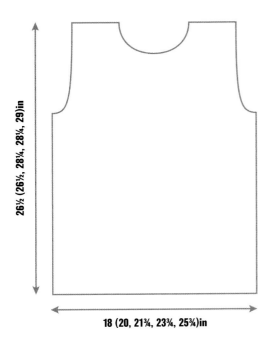

26½ (26½, 28¼, 28¼, 29)in

18 (20, 21¾, 23¾, 25¾)in

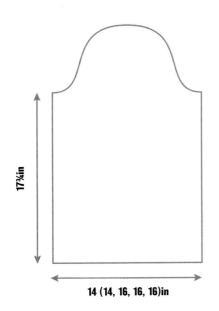

17¾in

14 (14, 16, 16, 16)in

Collar

Join right shoulder seam.

With right side facing, US 8 needles and yarn A, pick up and knit 12 (12, 13, 12, 12) stitches down left front neck, knit 17 (17, 19, 21, 21) stitches from holder at center front, pick up and knit 12 (12, 13, 12, 12) stitches up right front neck, pick up and knit 11 (11, 12, 11, 11) stitches down right back neck, knit 17 (17, 19, 21, 21) stitches from holder at back, pick up and knit 12 (12, 13, 12, 12) stitches up left back neck.
(81 (81, 89, 89, 89) stitches)
Change to US 10 needles.
Starting with row 1, continue in the chevron pattern as given for the Back and front alike, until the collar measures 11¾in, ending with a wrong-side row.
Bind off knitwise in yarn B.

Finish

Join left shoulder seam and collar edge, reversing seam half-way.
Sew on sleeves, placing center of sleeves to shoulder seams.
Join the side and sleeve seams.
Weave in ends.

MISKI
sweater with elongated neck-opening

The simple notion of using a different contrasting edging on a garment with a deep neck-opening, creates a sweater with a surprising detail.

MEASUREMENTS

To fit bust (suggested)	32–34	36–38	38–40	42–44	46–48	in
Actual measurement	37	39¼	41½	43¾	45¾	in
Length	30¼	30¼	31	32¼	32¼	in
Sleeve length	17¾	17¾	17¾	17¾	17¾	in

MATERIALS
Worsted (CYCA Medium #4) yarn
Mirasol Miski (100% Baby Llama; 82yd/50g):
yarn A, 16 (17, 17, 18, 18) skeins #115;
yarn B, 1 (1, 1, 2, 2) skeins #119.
(photographed in: yarn A, Black Beauty; yarn B, Orchid)

8 small buttons

NEEDLES
One pair of US 7 knitting needles
One pair of US 8 knitting needles
Knitter's sewing needle or tapestry needle

GAUGE
18 stitches and 28 rows to 4in square over garter stitch pattern using US 8 needles.

Back
With US 8 needles and yarn B, cast on 85 (90, 95, 100, 105) stitches.
Change to yarn A.

EDGE PATTERN
Row 1 (right side): Knit to end.
Row 2: K2, p1, [k4, p1] to last 2 stitches, k2.
These 2 rows form the edge pattern.
Repeat the last 2 rows until back measures 7¾ (7¾, 7¾, 9¾, 9¾)in from the cast-on edge, ending with a wrong-side row.

MAIN PATTERN
Row 1 (right side): K2, p1, [k4, p1] to last 2 stitches, k2.
Row 2: Knit to end.
These 2 rows form the main pattern.
Repeat the last 2 rows until back measures 21½ (21½, 21½, 22¾, 22¾)in from the cast-on edge, ending with a wrong-side row.

SHAPE ARMHOLES

Bind off 4 stitches at the beginning of the next 2 rows.

(77 (82, 87, 92, 97) stitches)

Decrease one stitch at each end of the next row and on every 4th row until 69 (74, 79, 84, 89) stitches remain.

Continue without shaping in main pattern until armhole measures 8¾ (8¾, 9½, 9½, 9½)in from start of armhole shaping, ending with a wrong-side row.

SHAPE SHOULDERS

Bind off 17 (19, 21, 22, 24) stitches at the beginning of the next 2 rows.

Place the remaining 35 (36, 37, 40, 41) stitches on a stitch holder.

Front

With US 8 needles and yarn B, cast on 85 (90, 95, 100, 105) stitches.

Change to yarn A.

EDGE PATTERN

Row 1 (right side): Knit to end.

Row 2: K2, p1, [k4, p1] to last 2 stitches, k2.

These 2 rows form the edge pattern.

Repeat the last 2 rows until front measures 7¾ (7¾, 7¾, 9¾, 9¾)in from the cast-on edge, ending with a wrong-side row.

Starting with row 1 of the main pattern given for Back, continue in the main pattern shaping left side as follows:

SHAPE LEFT SIDE

Next row: Work in main pattern until there are 42 (45, 47, 50, 52) stitches on the right hand needle, slip remaining stitches onto a stitch holder, turn and work in main pattern to end.

Continue in main pattern on these 42 (45, 47, 50, 52) stitches until front measures 21½ (21½, 21½, 22¾, 22¾)in from the cast-on edge, ending with a wrong-side row.

SHAPE ARMHOLE

Bind off 4 stitches at the beginning of the next row. *(38 (41, 43, 46, 48) stitches)*
Work one row in pattern.
Decrease one stitch at the armhole edge of the next row and on every 4th row until 34 (37, 39, 42, 44) stitches remain.
Continue without shaping in main pattern until armhole measures 6¼ (6¼, 7, 7, 7)in from start of armhole shaping, ending with a right-side row.

SHAPE LEFT NECK

Next row: Work 11 stitches in pattern, slip these stitches onto a stitch holder, work in pattern to end.
(23 (26, 28, 31, 33) stitches)
Work one row in pattern.
Decrease one stitch at the neck edge of the next row and on each of the following rows until 17 (19, 21, 22, 24) stitches remain.
Continue without shaping in main pattern, until armhole measures 8¾ (8¾, 9½, 9½, 9½)in from start of armhole shaping, ending with a wrong-side row.
Bind off.

SHAPE RIGHT SIDE

With right side facing, bind off
1 (0, 1, 0, 1) stitch, rejoin yarn to remaining 42 (45, 47, 50, 52) stitches, work in pattern to end.
Work as given for left side, reversing shapings.

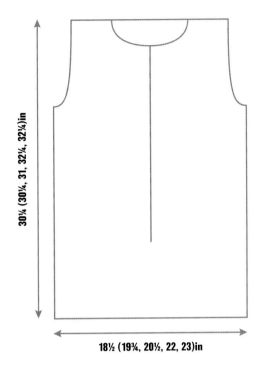

30¼ (30¼, 31, 32¼, 32¼)in

18½ (19¾, 20½, 22, 23)in

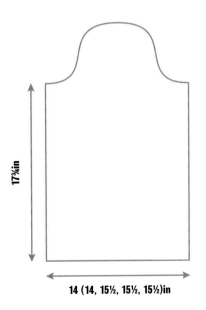

17¾in

14 (14, 15½, 15½, 15½)in

Sleeves

With US 8 needles and yarn B, cast on
65 (65, 70, 70, 70) stitches.
Change to yarn A.
Starting with row 1 of the main pattern as
given for the Back, continue in the main
pattern until sleeve measures 17¾in from the
cast-on edge, ending with a wrong-side row.

SHAPE TOP

Bind off 4 stitches at the beginning of the
next 2 rows.
(57 (57, 62, 62, 62) stitches)
Decrease one stitch at each end of the
next row and on every 4th row until 45 (45,
50, 50, 50) stitches remain.
Work 3 rows in pattern.
Decrease one stitch at each end of the
next row and on each of the alternate rows
until 35 (35, 40, 40, 40) stitches remain.
Work one row in pattern.
Decrease one stitch at each end of the next
row and on each of the following rows until
19 (19, 20, 20, 20) stitches remain.
Bind off 5 stitches at the beginning of the
next 2 rows. *(9 (9, 10, 10, 10) stitches)*
Bind off remaining stitches.

Left edging

Join shoulder seams.
With right side facing, US 7 needles and
yarn B, pick up and knit 105 stitches down
left front opening edge.
Knit one row.
Bind off.

Right edging

With right side facing, US 7 needles and
yarn B, pick up and knit 105 stitches up
right front opening edge.
Buttonhole row (wrong side): K9, [k2tog,
yo, k10] to end.
Bind off loosely over yo.

Neck

With right side facing, US 7 needles and
yarn B, pick up and knit 2 stitches from
edging, knit 11 stitches from holder at right
front, pick up and knit 17 stitches up right
front neck, knit 35 (36, 37, 40, 41) stitches
from holder at the back, pick up and knit 17
stitches down left front neck, knit 11 stitches
from holder at left front, pick up and knit 2
stitches from edging.
(95 (96, 97, 100, 101) stitches)
Knit one row.
Bind off.

Finish

Sew on sleeves, placing center of sleeves
to shoulder seams.
Join the side and sleeve seams.
Slip stitch edging ends into place with right
edging over left edging.
Position and sew buttons into place.
Weave in ends.

AKAPANA
sloppy-joe inspired, raglan sweater

This sweater is a hybrid—a sloppy-joe with shaping. It has the relaxed comfort of a sloppy-joe but texture and raglan shaping give it that unique hand-knitted feel.

MEASUREMENTS

To fit bust (suggested)	34–36	38–40	42–44	46–48	50–52	in
Actual measurement	42	46¼	50½	55	59½	in
Length	29½	30	30	31	31¼	in
Sleeve length	17¾	17¾	17¾	17¾	17¾	in

MATERIALS
Worsted (CYCA Medium #4) yarn
Mirasol Akapana (65% Baby Llama, 25% Merino Wool, 10% Donegal; 95yd/50g): 16 (17, 18, 19, 20) skeins #1304. (photographed in Moche Turquoise)

NEEDLES
One pair of US 6 knitting needles
One pair of US 7 knitting needles
Three stitch holders
Knitter's sewing needle or tapestry needle

GAUGE
18 stitches and 26 rows to 4in square over stockinette stitch using US 7 needles.

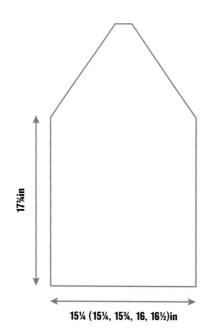

22½ (24¾, 27, 29¼, 31¼)in

29½ (30, 30, 31, 31¼)in

17¾in

15¼ (15¼, 15¾, 16, 16½)in

Back and front alike

With US 7 needles, cast on
116 (126, 136, 146, 156) stitches.
Rows 1 and 3 (right side): P29 (34, 39, 44, 49), k4, [p14, k4] 3 times, purl to end.
Row 2: K29 (34, 39, 44, 49), p4, *k1, [k1, p1, k1 all into the same stitch, p3tog] 3 times, k1, p4, repeat from * until there are 29 (34, 39, 44, 49) stitches, knit to end.
Row 4: K29 (34, 39, 44, 49), p4, *k1, [p3tog, k1, p1, k1 all into the same stitch] 3 times, k1, p4, repeat from * until there are 29 (34, 39, 44, 49) stitches, knit to end.
Repeat the last 4 rows until back measures 7¾in from the cast-on edge, ending with a 4th row.

Next row (right side): P29 (34, 39, 44, 49), k2tog, k2, [p14, k2tog, k2] 3 times, purl to end.
(112 (122, 132, 142, 152) stitches)
Row 1: K29 (34, 39, 44, 49), p3, *k1, [k1, p1, k1 all into the same stitch, p3tog] 3 times, k1, p3, repeat from * until there are 29 (34, 39, 44, 49) stitches, knit to end.
Rows 2 and 4 (right side): P29 (34, 39, 44, 49), k3, [p14, k3] 3 times, purl to end.
Row 3: K29 (34, 39, 44, 49), p3, *k1, [p3tog, k1, p1, k1 all into the same stitch] 3 times, k1, p3, repeat from * until there are 29 (34, 39, 44, 49) stitches, knit to end.
Repeat the last 4 rows until back measures 15in from the cast-on edge, ending with a 3rd row.

Next row (right side): P29 (34, 39, 44, 49), k2tog, k1, [p14, k2tog, k1] 3 times, purl to end.
(108 (118, 128, 138, 148) stitches)
Row 1: K29 (34, 39, 44, 49), p2, *k1, [k1, p1, k1 all into the same stitch, p3tog] 3 times, k1, p2, repeat from * until there are 29 (34, 39, 44, 49) stitches, knit to end.
Rows 2 and 4 (right side): P29 (34, 39, 44, 49), k2, [p14, k2] 3 times, purl to end.

Row 3: K29 (34, 39, 44, 49), p2, *k1, [p3tog, k1, p1, k1 all into the same stitch] 3 times, k1, p2, repeat from * until there are 29 (34, 39, 44, 49) stitches, knit to end.
Repeat the last 4 rows until back measures 20½in from the cast-on edge, ending with a wrong-side row.

SHAPE RAGLANS

Decrease row (right side): K1, k2togtbl, work in the pattern to last 3 stitches, k2tog, k1.
(106 (116, 126, 136, 146) stitches)

Next row: P2 (2, 1, 1, 1), [p2tog] 0 (0, 1, 1, 1) times work in the pattern to last 2 (2, 3, 3, 3) stitches, [p2togtbl] 0 (0, 1,1,1) times, p2 (2,1,1,1).
(106 (116, 124, 134, 144) stitches)
These 2 rows set the position of the decrease, with stockinette stitch panel.

SIZE EXTRA SMALL ONLY

Decrease one stitch as set above on each end of the 3rd row and following 4th row.

SIZE SMALL ONLY

Decrease one stitch as set above on each end of the 3rd row only.

SIZES MEDIUM, LARGE, AND EXTRA LARGE ONLY

Decrease one stitch as set above on each end of the next row only.

ALL SIZES

Work one row in the pattern.
(102 (114, 122, 132, 142) stitches)
Decrease one stitch as set above at each end of the next row and on each of the alternate rows, until 52 (58, 62, 66, 74) stitches remain, ending with a wrong-side row.
Place the remaining stitches on a holder.

Sleeves

With US 7 needles, cast on 70 (70, 72, 74, 76) stitches.
Starting with a purl row, continue in reverse stockinette stitch until sleeve measure 17¾in from the cast-on edge, ending with a wrong-side row.

SHAPE RAGLANS

Decrease one stitch as set for Back on the next row and on each of the alternate rows, until 10 (8, 8, 4, 4) stitches remain.
Leave these stitches on a holder.

Neck edging

Join raglan seams leaving left front open.
With right side facing and US 6 needles, pick up and knit 52 (58, 62, 66, 74) stitches from center front neck, knit 10 (8, 8, 4, 4) stitches from holder at sleeve and pick up and knit 52 (58, 62, 66, 74) stitches from holder from the back, knit 10 (8, 8, 4, 4) stitches from holder at sleeve.
(124 (132, 140, 140, 156) stitches)

Next row: [K4, k2tog] to last 4 (0, 2, 2, 0) stitches, k4 (0, 2, 2, 0).
(104 (110, 117, 117, 130) stitches)
Knit 4 rows.
Bind off.

Finish

Join the left raglan and neck edging seam.
Join the side and sleeve seams.
Weave in ends.

NUNA
wide-neck sweater with ruffly-stripes

This is a striped sweater with a difference. Each stripe-band uses one of two needle sizes and increases and decreases to create ruffly-stripes. There are a few moments where concentration is needed in this pattern but I feel the end results makes it worth it.

MEASUREMENTS

To fit bust (suggested)	32–34	34–36	38–40	40–42	44–46	in
Actual measurement	36½	38½	42½	44½	47¾	in
Length	30¾	30¾	31½	32¼	32¼	in
Sleeve length	17¾	17¾	17¾	17¾	17¾	in

MATERIALS
DK (CYCA Light #3) yarn
Mirasol Nuna (40% Merino Wool, 40% Silk, 20% Bamboo; 191 yd/50g):
yarn A, 3 (3, 4, 4, 4) skeins #1001;
yarn B, 3 (3, 4, 4, 4) skeins #1002.
(photographed in: yarn A, Ebony; yarn B, Warm Grey)

NEEDLES
One pair of US 3 knitting needles
One pair of US 2/3 knitting needles
Knitter's sewing needle or tapestry needle

GAUGE
24 stitches and 34 rows to 4in square over pattern using US 3 needles.

81

Back and front alike

With US 2/3 needles and yarn A, cast on
112 (118, 130, 136, 146) stitches.

RIB PATTERN

Row 1 (right side): K0 (2, 2, 0, 2),
[p2, k2] to end.

Row 2: [P2, k2] to last 0 (2, 2, 0, 2) stitches,
p0 (2, 2, 0, 2).

These 2 rows form the rib pattern.

Repeat the last 2 rows with yarn A only until
work measures 2in from the cast-on edge,
ending with a right-side row.

MAIN PATTERN

With US 2/3 needles work rows
1–8 as follows:

Row 1 (wrong side): With yarn A, purl to end.

Row 2 (right side): With yarn A, knit into
back and front of all stitches.

(224 (236, 260, 272, 292) stitches)

Rows, 3, 5, and 7: With yarn A, purl to end.

Rows 4 and 6: With yarn A, knit to end.

Row 8: With yarn A, [k2tog] to end.

(112 (118, 130, 136, 146) stitches)

With US 3 needles work rows 9–14 as
follows:

Row 9: With yarn B, purl to end.

Rows 10, 12, and 14: With yarn B,
knit to end.

Rows 11 and 13: With yarn B, purl to end.

These 14 rows form the pattern.

Continue in the pattern until the work
measures approximately 21½in from the
cast-on edge, ending after row 6 has been
completed and with a right-side row.

(224 (236, 260, 272, 292) stitches)

SHAPE RAGLANS

Decrease one stitch at each end of the next
row and 8 (8, 6, 6, 1) of the following 4th
rows, then on the following 12 (12, 20, 23,
23) alternate rows.

Work one row in pattern, ending after row
8 (8, 2, 8, 8) has been completed with a
right-side row.

(80 (86, 174, 90, 92) stitches)

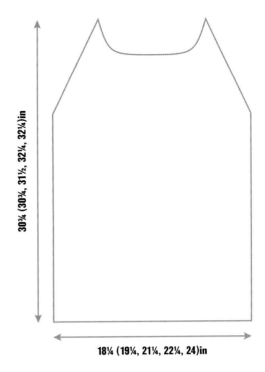

30¾ (30¾, 31½, 32¼, 32¼)in

18¼ (19¼, 21¼, 22¼, 24)in

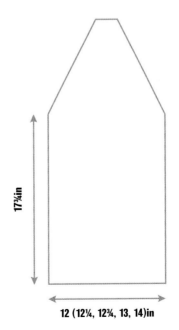

17¾in

12 (12¼, 12¾, 13, 14)in

SHAPE RIGHT NECK AND RAGLAN

Next row: P2tog, p13 (13, 25, 13, 13), turn and leave remaining 65 (71, 147, 75, 77) stitches on a stitch holder.

Work one row in pattern.

Decrease one stitch at each end of the next row and on each of the alternate rows until 1 (1, 2, 1, 1) stitches remain.

Next row: K1 (1, 0, 1, 1), [k2tog] 0 (0, 1, 0, 0) times.

Fasten off remaining stitch.

With wrong-side facing, leave center 50 (56, 120, 60, 62) stitches on a stitch holder, rejoin yarn to remaining 15 (15, 27, 15, 15) stitches, purl to the last 2 stitches, p2tog. *(14 (14, 26, 14, 14) stitches)*

Work one row in pattern.

Decrease one stitch at each end of the next row and on each of the alternate rows until 1 (1, 2, 1, 1) stitches remain.

Next row: K1 (1, 0, 1, 1), [k2tog] 0 (0, 1, 0, 0) times.

Fasten off remaining stitch.

Sleeves

With US 2/3 needles and yarn A, cast on 72 (74, 78, 80, 86) stitches.

Starting with row 1 of the rib pattern for the Back and front, work as given until sleeve measures approximately 17¾in from the cast-on edge, ending after row 6 of main pattern and with a right-side row. *(144 (148, 156, 160, 172) stitches)*

SHAPE RAGLAN

Decrease one stitch at each end of the next row and 2 (2, 2, 7, 2) of the following 4th rows, then on the following 33 (33, 37, 30, 40) alternate rows.

Work one row in pattern, ending after row 12 (12, 6, 12, 12) of main pattern and with a right-side row. *(16 (18, 32, 20, 18) stitches)*

Place the remaining stitches on a stitch holder.

Neck edging

Join the raglan seams, leaving front left seam open.

With right side facing, US 2/3 needles and yarn A, pick up and knit 14 stitches down left front neck, work across 50 (56, 120, 60, 62) stitches from the stitch holder at the front as follows: k50 (56, 0, 60, 62), [k2tog] 0 (0, 60, 0, 0) times, pick up and knit 14 stitches up right front neck, work across 16 (18, 32, 20, 18) stitches from the stitch holder at the top of the right sleeve as follows: k16 (18, 0, 20, 18), [k2tog] 0 (0, 16, 0, 0) times, pick up and knit 14 stitches down right back neck, work across 50 (56, 120, 60, 62) stitches from the stitch holder at the back as follows: k50 (56, 0, 60, 62), [k2tog] 0 (0, 60, 0, 0) times, pick up and knit 14 stitches up left back neck, work across 16 (18, 32, 20, 18) stitches from the stitch holder at the top of the left sleeve as follows: k16 (18, 0, 20, 18), [k2tog] 0 (0, 16, 0, 0) times. *(188 (204, 208, 216, 216) stitches)*

Rib row: [K2, p2] to end.

This row forms the rib pattern.

Repeat last row until neck edging measures 2¼in, ending with a wrong-side row.

Bind off.

Finish

Join left raglan and neck edging seam.

Sew together sleeve and side seams.

Weave in ends.

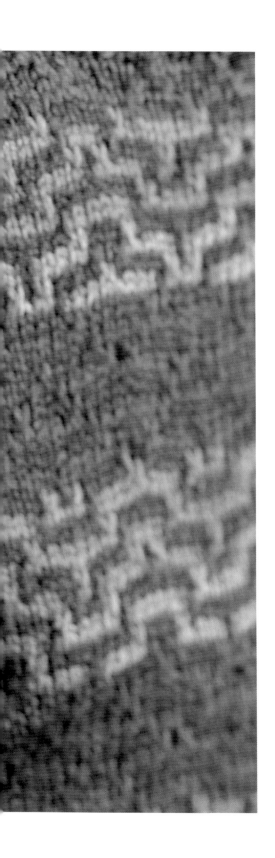

3 Dresses and Tunics

sleeveless dress
page 88

lace, short-sleeved dress
page 92

ribbed, sleeveless tank top
page 96

elongated, v-neck, sleeveless dress
page 100

long, v-necked vest
page 104

SAMP'A
sleeveless dress

The stitch pattern at the top of this dress not only creates a gentle ripple texture in the fabric and beautiful edge detail but gives the illusion of separate, small cap sleeves.

MEASUREMENTS

To fit bust (suggested)	32–38	40–46	in
Actual measurement	42½	51¾	in
Length	27½	27½	in

MATERIALS

DK (CYCA Light #3) yarn
Mirasol Samp'a (100% Organic Cotton;
120yd/50g):
10 (12) skeins #608.
(photographed in Hickory)

NEEDLES

One pair of US 5 knitting needles
Cable needle
One stitch holder
Two markers or safety pins
Knitter's sewing needle or tapestry needle

GAUGE

24 stitches and 32 rows to 4in square over
cable pattern using US 5 needles.

SPECIAL ABBREVIATIONS

T4B: Slip next 2 stitches onto cable needle
and hold at back, k2 from left-hand needle,
p2 from cable needle.

T4F: Slip next 2 stitches onto cable needle
and hold at front, p2 from left-hand needle,
k2 from cable needle.

Back and front alike

With US 5 needles, cast on
130 (158) stitches.

RIB PATTERN

Row 1 (right side): P6, k6, *p4, [k2, p4] 3
times, k6, repeat from * to last 6 stitches, p6.
Row 2: K6, p6, [k4, p14, k4, p6] to last
6 stitches, k6.
These 2 rows form the rib pattern.
Repeat the last 2 rows until back measures
17¾in from the cast-on edge, ending with a
wrong-side row.

CABLE PATTERN

Row 1 (right side): P6, k6, *p4, [k2, p4] 3
times, k6, repeat from * to last 6 stitches, p6.
Row 2: K6, p6, [k4, p14, k4, p6] to last
6 stitches, k6.

Row 3: P4, T4B, k2, *[T4F, p2] twice, k2,
[p2, T4B] twice, k2, repeat from * to last
8 stitches, T4F, p4.
Row 4: K4, [p10, k4] to end.
Row 5: P2, T4B, p2, k2, *[p2, T4F] twice,
k2, [T4B, p2] twice, k2, repeat from * to
last 8 stitches, p2, T4F, p2.
Row 6: K2, p14, [k4, p6, k4, p14] to last
2 stitches, k2.
Row 7: P2, *[k2, p4] 3 times, k6, p4,
repeat from * to last 16 stitches, k2, [p4,
k2] twice, p2.
Row 8: Repeat row 6.
Row 9: P2, T4F, p2, k2, *[p2, T4B] twice,
k2, [T4F, p2] twice, k2, repeat from * to last
8 stitches, p2, T4B, p2.
Row 10: Repeat row 4.
Row 11: P4, T4F, k2, *[T4B, p2] twice, k2,
[p2, T4F] twice, k2, repeat from * to last
8 stitches, T4B, p4.
Row 12: Repeat row 2.
These 12 rows form the cable pattern.

Repeat these last 12 rows until work measures 26in from the cast-on edge, ending with a wrong-side row.
Keeping pattern correct.

SHAPE NECK

Continue keeping pattern correct.

Next row: Work 38 (52) stitches in pattern, place the remaining stitches on a stitch holder, turn.

Work in cable pattern until 12 rows have been completed.

Bind off.

SHAPE NECK

With right side facing, rejoin yarn to remaining stitches, bind off center 54 stitches, work in pattern to end.

Work to match other neck.

Finish

Join shoulder seams.

Place markers 7¾in down from shoulder seams and join the side seams beneath markers.

Weave in ends.

27½in

22 (26)in

samp'a: sleeveless dress

TUPA
lace, short-sleeved dress

The lace on the top of this dress is a joy. And nothing complemented it better than the simplicity of stockinette (stocking) stitch.

MEASUREMENTS

To fit bust (suggested)	32–34	36–38	40–42	44–46	46–48	in
Actual	37	40¼	43¼	46½	49½	in
Length	30	30	30¾	30¾	31½	in
Sleeve length	4¾	4¾	4¾	4¾	4¾	in

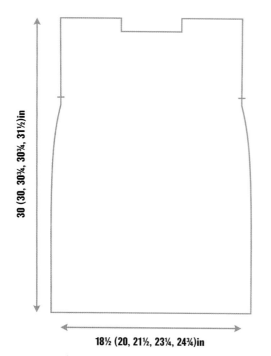

30 (30, 30¾, 30¾, 31½)in

18½ (20, 21½, 23¼, 24¾)in

MATERIALS
DK (CYCA Light #3) yarn
Mirasol Tupa (50% Merino Wool, 50% Silk; 137yd/50g):
8 (9, 9, 10, 10) skeins #810.
(photographed in Dark Auburn)

NEEDLES
One pair of US 5 knitting needles
One pair of US 6 knitting needles
Two stitch holders
Two markers or safety pins
Knitter's sewing needle or tapestry needle

GAUGE
20 stitches and 30 rows to 4in square over lace pattern using US 6 needles.

22 stitches and 30 rows to 4in square over stockinette stitch using US 6 needles.

Back and front alike

With US 6 needles, cast on
114 (124, 134, 144, 154) stitches.
Starting with a knit row, work in stockinette
stitch until work measures 22 (22, 22¾,
22¾, 23½)in from the cast-on edge, ending
with a wrong-side row.

Decrease row: K6, [k3, k2tog] to last
8 stitches, k8.
(94 (102, 110, 118, 126) stitches)
Purl one row.

LACE PATTERN

Row 1 (right side): K2, [k2tog, k1, yo, k1,
sl1, k1, psso, k2] to last 4 stitches, k4.
Row 2 and every alt pattern row: Purl to end.
Row 3: K1, k2tog, k1, yo, [k1, yo, k1, sl1,
k1, psso, k2tog, k1, yo] to last 2 stitches, k2.
Row 5: K3, yo, [k3, yo, k1, sl1, k1, psso,
k1, yo] to last 3 stitches, k3.
Row 7: K5, [k2tog, k1, yo, k1, sl1, k1,
psso, k2] to last 2 stitches, k2.
Row 9: K4, *k2tog, k1, [yo, k1] twice, sl1,
k1, psso, repeat from * to last 3 stitches, k3.
Row 11: K3, k2tog, [k1, yo, k3, yo, k1,
k2tog] to last 2 stitches, k2.
Row 12: Purl to end.
These 12 rows form the lace pattern.
Repeat the last 12 rows 3 times.

SHAPE ONE NECK AND SHOULDER

Next row: Work pattern until there are 30
(30, 38, 38, 38) stitches, place remaining
stitches on a stitch holder, turn, purl to end.
Work 10 rows in pattern.
Bind off.

SHAPE OTHER NECK AND SHOULDER

With right side facing, leave center 34 (42,
34, 42, 50) stitches on the stitch holder,
rejoin yarn to 30 (30, 38, 38, 38) stitches.
Work to match one neck and shoulder.
Bind off.

Sleeves

With US 6 needles, cast on
78 (86, 86, 94, 94) stitches.
Purl one row.
Starting with row 1 of the lace pattern for the
Back, continue in pattern until sleeve
measures 4¾in from the cast-on edge,
ending with a wrong-side row.
Bind off.

Neck edging

Join right shoulder seam.
With right side facing and US 5 needles, pick
up and knit 9 stitches down left front neck,
knit 34 (42, 34, 42, 50) stitches from stitch
holder at front, pick up and knit 9 stitches
up right front neck, pick up and knit 9
stitches down back neck, pick up and knit
34 (42, 34, 42, 50) stitches from stitch
holder at back, pick up and knit 9 stitches
up back neck.
(104 (120, 104, 120, 136) stitches)
Bind off on a wrong-side row.

Finish

Join left shoulder seam and neck edging.
Place markers 7¾ (8¼, 8¼, 9, 9)in down
from shoulder seams.
Sew on sleeves, placing center of sleeves to
shoulder seams and easing edge to markers.
Join sleeve seams and side seams beneath
the markers.
Weave in ends.

K'ACHA
ribbed, sleeveless tank top

Experimenting with stripe repeats is always fun and the rib softens the stripe edge and helps to transform the fabric into something unique.

MEASUREMENTS

To fit bust	32–34	36–38	38–40	42–44	46–48	in
Actual measurement	41¾	45	48	51	54¼	in
Length	25½	25½	26¼	26¼	27½	in
Sleeve length	1	1	1	1	1	in

MATERIALS

DK (CYCA Light #3) yarn

Mirasol K'acha (60% Fine Merino Wool, 25% Alpaca, 15% Silk; 98yd/50g):

yarn A, 2 (3, 3, 4, 4) skeins #1201;
yarn B, 2 (3, 3, 4, 4) skeins #1202;
yarn C, 1 (2, 2, 3, 3) skeins #1207;
yarn D, 1 (2, 2, 3, 3) skeins #1206;
yarn E, 1 (2, 2, 3, 3) skeins #1204;
yarn F, 1 (2, 2, 3, 3) skeins #1205.

(photographed in: yarn A, Cinnamon; yarn B, Royal Purple; yarn C, Vintage Green; yarn D, Deep Navy; yarn E, Magenta Magic; yarn F, Dark Chocolate)

NEEDLES

One pair of US 5 knitting needles
One pair of US 6 knitting needles
One stitch holder
Two markers or safety pins
Knitter's sewing needle or tapestry needle

GAUGE

20 stitches and 26 rows to 4in square over rib pattern when slightly stretched using US 6 needles.

STRIPE PATTERN

With yarn C, work 1 row.
With yarn D, work 1 row.
With yarn B, work 2 rows.
With yarn E, work 1 row.
With yarn F, work 1 row.
With yarn A, work 2 rows.
With yarn D, work 1 row.
With yarn C, work 1 row.
With yarn B, work 2 rows.
With yarn F, work 1 row.
With yarn E, work 1 row.
With yarn A, work 2 rows.
These 16 rows form the stripe pattern.
Repeat these 16 rows throughout.

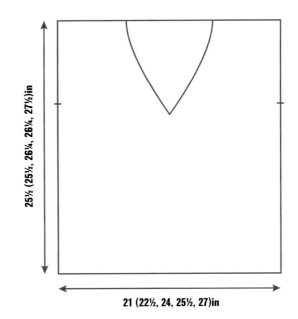

25½ (25½, 26¼, 26¼, 27½)in

21 (22½, 24, 25½, 27)in

Back

With US 6 needles and yarn A, cast on 106 (114, 122, 130, 138) stitches.

RIB PATTERN

Row 1 (right side): K2, [p6, k2] to end.
Row 2: P2, [k6, p2] to end.
These 2 rows form the rib pattern.
Starting with the first row of the stripe pattern, work in the rib pattern and stripe pattern until back measures 25½ (25½, 26¼, 26¼, 27½)in from the cast-on edge, ending with a wrong-side row.

SHAPE SHOULDERS

Bind off 32 (36, 39, 42, 45) stitches at the beginning of next 2 rows.
Place center 42 (42, 44, 46, 48) stitches on a stitch holder.

Front

Work as given for the Back until the front measures 15¾ (15¾, 16½, 16½,17¾)in from the cast-on edge, ending with a wrong-side row.

SHAPE LEFT NECK

Next row: Work pattern until there are 53 (57, 61, 65, 69) stitches on right-hand needle, place remaining stitches on a stitch holder, turn.

Next row: K3 (1, 3, 1, 3), p2 (0, 2, 0, 2), [k6, p2] to end.

Decrease row (right side): Work in pattern to last 7 stitches, p2togtbl, k2 (0, 2, 0, 2), p3 (5, 3, 5, 3).

(52 (56, 60, 64, 68) stitches)

The last decrease row sets the position of the decrease stitch.

Keeping pattern correct, decrease one stitch at the neck edge on each of the alternate rows until 40 (44, 46, 48, 50) stitches remain. Work 3 rows in pattern.

Decrease one stitch at the neck edge of the next row and on every 4th row, until 32 (36, 39, 42, 45) stitches remain.

Continue without shaping in rib pattern and striped pattern until front measures 25½ (25½, 26¼, 26¼, 27½)in from the cast-on edge, ending with a wrong-side row. Bind off.

SHAPE RIGHT NECK

With right side facing, rejoin yarn to remaining 53 (57, 61, 65, 69) stitches, work in pattern to end.

Next row: [P2, k6] to last 5 (1, 5, 1, 5) stitches, p2 (1, 2, 1, 2), k3 (0, 3, 0, 3).

Decrease row (right side): P3 (5, 3, 5, 3), k2 (0, 2, 0, 2), p2tog, pattern to end.

(52 (56, 60, 64, 68) stitches)

This last decrease row sets the position of the decrease stitch.

Work to match left neck, reversing shaping.

Neck edging

Join right shoulder seam.

With right side facing, US 5 needles, and yarn A, pick up and knit 51 stitches down left front neck, pick up and knit 51 stitches up right front neck, pick up and knit 42 (42, 44, 46, 48) stitches from stitch holder at back. *(144 (144, 146, 148, 150) stitches)*

Next row: Knit 90 (90, 92, 94, 96) stitches, k2togtbl, k2, k2tog, knit to end. Bind off on wrong-side row.

Armhole edging

Join left shoulder and neck edging seam. Place markers 7¾ (8¼, 8¾, 9, 9½)in down from shoulder seams.

With right side facing, US 5 needles, and yarn A, pick up and knit 44 (46, 48, 50, 52) stitches from marker up one side of armhole edge, pick up and knit 44 (46, 48, 50, 52) stitches down other side of armhole edge to the marker.

(88 (92, 96, 100, 104) stitches)

Knit one row.

Bind off on wrong-side row.

Finish

Join the side and armhole edges.
Weave in ends.

NUNA
elongated, v-neck, sleeveless dress

The combination of this stitch technique and the fine yarn means this garment can easily be worn, over a vest top, in summer months too.

MEASUREMENTS

To fit bust (suggested)	34–36	38–40	42–44	44–46	48–50	in
Actual measurement	38	41¾	45¼	49	52¾	in
Length	33	33	33¾	33¾	34½	in

MATERIALS
DK (CYCA Light #3) yarn
Mirasol Nuna (40% Merino Wool, 40% Silk, 20% Bamboo; 191 yd/50g):
yarn A, 5 (6, 6, 7, 7) skeins #1011;
yarn B, 2 (2, 3, 3, 3) skeins #1010.
(photographed in: yarn A, Maya Blue; yarn B, Myrtle)

NEEDLES
One pair of US 3 knitting needles
One stitch holder
Two markers or safety pins
Knitter's sewing needle or tapestry needle

GAUGE
26 stitches and 32 rows to 4in square over main pattern using US 3 needles.

Note: The front of this dress uses the intarsia technique. It is the simplest form of intarsia. When joining in the second yarn, twist the two yarns around each other on the wrong side to avoid gaps. The twist is, again, very basic and happens just once by placing the yarn that has just been used over the yarn that is to be used, the yarn to be used is then brought up, thus creating a little twist.

Back
With US 3 needles and yarn A, cast on 126 (138, 150, 162, 174) stitches.
MAIN PATTERN
Row 1 (right side): With yarn A, knit to end.
Row 2: With yarn A, p1, k1, [p5, k1] to last 4 stitches, p4.
These 2 rows form the main pattern.
Repeat the last 2 rows with yarn A only until back measures 15¾ (15¾, 16¼, 16½, 16½)in from the cast-on edge, ending with wrong-side row.

RIB PATTERN

Row 1: With yarn B, [k3, p3] to end.

Row 2: With yarn B, [k1, p1] to end.

These 2 rows form the rib pattern.

Repeat the last 2 rows until back measures 19 (19, 19¼, 19¾, 19¾)in from the cast-on edge, ending with a wrong-side row.

Starting with row 1 of the main pattern and using yarn A only, continue in the main pattern until back measures 33 (33, 33¾, 33¾ 34½)in from the cast-on edge, ending with a wrong-side row.

SHAPE SHOULDERS

Bind off 37 (43, 47, 53, 57) stitches at the beginning of next 2 rows.

Bind off remaining 52 (52, 56, 56, 60) stitches.

Front

Work as given for the Back until front measures 19 (19, 19¼, 19¾, 19¾)in from the cast-on edge, ending with a wrong-side row.

SHAPE LEFT NECK

Next row: With yarn A, k39 (45, 51, 57, 63), with yarn B, work 24 stitches in pattern, place remaining stitches on a stitch holder, turn.

Next row (wrong side): With yarn B, pattern 24 stitches, with yarn A, purl to end.

Next row (right side): With yarn A, knit to last 24 stitches, with yarn B, work in pattern to end.

These 2 rows set the position of the ribbing. Work one row in pattern.

Decrease row (right side): With yarn A, knit to last 26 stitches, k2togtbl, with yarn B, work in pattern to end.

Decrease one stitch as set above at the neck edge of the next row and on every 4th row until 37 (43, 47, 53, 57) stitches remain.

Continue without shaping in pattern until front measures 33 (33, 33¾, 33¾, 34½)in from the cast-on edge, ending with a wrong-side row.

Bind off.

SHAPE RIGHT NECK

With right side facing, rejoin yarn to remaining 63 (69, 75, 81, 87) stitches, with yarn B, work in pattern for 24 stitches, with yarn A, knit to end.

Work to match left neck, reversing shaping.

Armhole edging

Join shoulder seams.

Place markers 7¾ (8¼, 8¾, 9, 9½)in down from shoulder seams.

With right side facing, US 3 needles, and yarn B, pick up and knit 48 (51, 54, 57, 60) stitches from marker up one side of armhole edge, pick up and knit 48 (51, 54, 57, 60) stitches down other side of armhole edge to the marker.

(96 (102, 108, 114, 120) stitches)

RIB PATTERN

Row 1 (wrong side): [K1, p1] to end.

Row 2: [K3, p3] to end.

Work the rib row 1 once more.

Bind off in rib pattern.

Finish

Join the side and armhole edging seams.

Weave in ends.

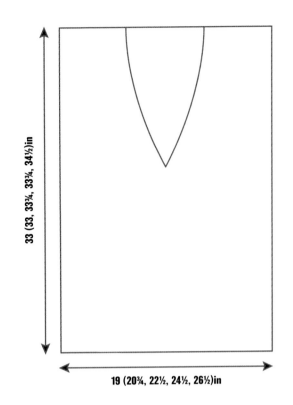

33 (33, 33¾, 33¾, 34½)in

19 (20¾, 22½, 24½, 26½)in

NUNA
long, v-necked vest

This vest has so many elements to enjoy. Both the slip stitch technique and the striping are simple to do but create a fabric that looks more complicated.

MEASUREMENTS

To fit bust	34–36	38–40	42–44	44–46	48–50	in
Actual measurement	39½	43	46¾	50¾	54½	in
Length	30¼	30¾	31¾	32½	32¾	in

MATERIALS

DK (CYCA Light #3) yarn
Mirasol Nuna (40% Merino Wool, 40% Silk, 20% Bamboo; 191 yd/50g):
yarn A, 3 (4, 4, 5, 5) skeins #1005;
yarn B, 1 (2, 2, 2, 3) skeins #1008;
yarn C, 1 (2, 2, 3, 3) skeins #1004;
yarn D, 1 (1, 1, 2, 2) skeins #1011.
(photographed in: yarn A, Prussian Blue; yarn B, Ocean Blue; yarn C, Cardinal Red; yarn D, Maya Blue)

NEEDLES

One pair of US 2/3 knitting needles
One pair of US 3 knitting needles
Two stitch holders
Knitter's sewing needle or tapestry needle

GAUGE

25 stitches and 32 rows to 4in square over pattern using US 3 needles.

STRIPE PATTERN

With yarn A, work 2 rows.
With yarn B, work 2 rows.
With yarn A, work 2 rows.
With yarn B, work 2 rows.
With yarn A, work 2 rows.
With yarn B, work 2 rows.
With yarn A, work 2 rows.
With yarn C, work 2 rows.
With yarn A, work 2 rows.
With yarn C, work 2 rows.
With yarn A, work 2 rows.
With yarn C, work 2 rows.
With yarn A, work 2 rows.
With yarn C, work 2 rows.
With yarn A, work 2 rows.
With yarn D, work 2 rows.
With yarn A, work 2 rows.
With yarn D, work 2 rows.

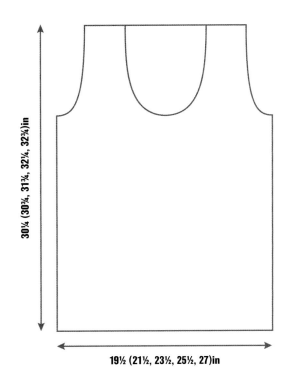

30¼ (30¾, 31¾, 32¼, 32¾)in

19½ (21½, 23½, 25½, 27)in

Back

With US 2/3 needles with yarn A, cast on
124 (136, 148, 160, 172) stitches.

RIB PATTERN

Row 1: [P2, k2] to end.

This row forms the rib patt.

Repeat the last row with yarn A only until the
back measures 4in from the cast-on edge,
ending with right-side row.

Purl one row, increase one stitch in the center
of the row.

(125 (137, 149, 161, 173) stitches)

Change to US 3 needles.

Starting with row 1 of the stripe pattern, work
the stripe pattern throughout:

SLIP STITCH PATTERN

Row 1 (right side): K4, [sl1, k7, sl1, k3] to
last stitch, k1.

Row 2: P4, [sl1, p7, sl1, p3] to last stitch, p1.

Row 3: K5, [sl1, k5] to end.

Row 4: P5, [sl1, p5] to end.

Row 5: K6, sl1, k3, sl1, [k7, sl1, k3, sl1] to
last 6 stitches, k6.

Row 6: P6, sl1, p3, sl1, [p7, sl1, p3, sl1] to
last 6 stitches, p6.

Row 7: K2, sl1, k4, sl1, k1, sl1, *[k4, sl1]
twice, k1, sl1; repeat from * to last 7 stitches,
k4, sl1, k2.

Row 8: P2, sl1, p4, sl1, p1, sl1, *[p4, sl1]
twice, p1, sl1; repeat from * to last 7 stitches,
p4, sl1, p2.

Row 9: [K1, sl1] twice, *[k4, sl1] twice, k1,
sl1; repeat from * to last stitch, k1.

Row 10: [P1, sl1] twice, *[p4, sl1] twice,
p1, sl1; repeat from * to last stitch, p1.

These 10 rows form the slip stitch pattern.
Repeat these 10 rows with the striped pattern
until back measures 21½ (22, 22½, 22¾,
23¼)in from the cast-on edge, ending with
a wrong-side row.

SHAPE ARMHOLES

Bind off 5 stitches at the beginning of the
next 2 rows.

(115 (127, 139, 151, 163) stitches)

Decrease row: Work 3 stitches in pattern,
sl1, k1, psso, work in pattern to last 5 stitches,
k2tog, work in pattern to the end.

(113 (125, 137, 149, 161) stitches)

This row sets the position of the decrease.
Decrease one stitch as set above at each end
of each alternate row, 6 times.

(101 (113, 125, 137, 149) stitches)

Decrease one stitch as set above at each end
of every 4th row, 6 times.

(89 (101, 113, 125, 137) stitches)

Continue without shaping in slip stitch
pattern and striped pattern until armhole
measures 8¾ (8¾, 9½, 9½, 9½)in from
start of armhole shaping, ending with a
wrong-side row.

SHAPE SHOULDERS

Bind off 19 (24, 29, 34, 39) stitches at the
beginning of next 2 rows.

Place remaining 51 (53, 55, 57, 59)
stitches on a stitch holder.

Front

Work as given for the Back until Shape
armholes, ending with a wrong-side row.

(125 (137, 149, 161, 173) stitches)

SHAPE LEFT NECK AND ARMHOLE

Next row: Bind off 5 stitches, work in pattern
until there are 45 (50, 55, 60, 65) stitches
on right-hand needle, place remaining stitches
on a stitch holder, turn.

Work one row in pattern.

Decrease one stitch at position set for Back
at each end of the next row and on each of
the alternate rows until 31 (36, 41, 46, 51)
stitches remain.

Work 3 rows in pattern.

Decrease one stitch at each end of the
next row and on every 4th row until 19 (24,
29, 34, 39) stitches remain.

Continue without shaping in slip stitch and stripe pattern until armhole measures 8¾ (8¾, 9½, 9½, 9½)in from start of armhole shaping, ending with a wrong-side row. Bind off.

SHAPE RIGHT NECK AND ARMHOLE

With right side facing, leave center 25 (27, 29, 31, 33) stitches on the stitch holder, rejoin yarn to remaining 50 (55, 60, 65, 70) stitches, work in pattern to end.

Bind off 5 stitches at the beginning of the next row.

Work to match left neck and armhole.

Neck edging

Join right shoulder seam.

With right side facing, US 2/3 needles and yarn A, pick up and knit 72 (72, 76, 76, 76) stitches down left front neck, knit 25 (27, 29, 31, 33) stitches from stitch holder at front increasing or decreasing one stitch evenly to make 26 (26, 30, 30, 34) stitches at center front, pick up and knit 73 (73, 77, 77, 77) stitches up right front neck and pick up and knit 51 (53, 55, 57, 59) stitches from stitch holder at back.

(222 (224, 238, 240, 246) stitches)

RIB PATTERN

Row 1 (wrong side): P2 (0, 2, 0, 2), [k2, p2] 30 (31, 32, 33, 33) times, k4, p2, [k2, p2] 5 (5, 6, 6, 7) times, k4, [p2, k2] to last 2 (0, 2, 0, 2) stitches, p2.

This row sets the rib patt.

Row 2: Rib to p4, p2tog, rib to next p4 then, p2, p2togtbl, rib to end.

Row 3: Rib to k3, k2togtbl, rib to next k3 then, k1, k2tog, rib to end.

Bind off in rib.

Armhole edging

Join left shoulder and neck edging seam.

With right side facing, US 2/3 needles, and yarn A, pick up and knit 77 (77, 81, 81, 81) stitches up one side of armhole edge, pick up and knit 77 (77, 81, 81, 81) stitches down other side of armhole.

(154 (154, 162, 162, 162) stitches)

RIB PATTERN

Row 1 (wrong side): P2, [k2, p2] to end.

Row 2: K2, [p2, k2] to end.

Repeat row 1 of rib once more.

Bind off in rib.

Finish

Join the side and armhole seams.

Weave in ends.

4

Hats, Scarves, and Mittens

slouchy socks
page 112

extra long, chunky scarf
page 114

seed stitch, floppy hat
page 116

mock-cable beret
page 118

mittens with finger-flap
page 120

fingerless gloves
page 124

lace, skinny scarf
page 126

slouchy socks

These socks have a cozy feel. Knitted socks that are a little bit too big for the foot are perfect for lazing around in at home.

SIZE
To fit shoe size US 6–9

MATERIALS
DK (CYCA Light #3) yarn
Mirasol Tupa (50% Merino Wool, 50% Silk; 137yd/50g):
Three skeins #814.
(photographed in Electrical Purple)

NEEDLES
Set of 4 double pointed US 6 knitting needles
Cable needle
Knitter's sewing needle or tapestry needle

GAUGE
22 stitches and 28 rows 4in square over pattern using US 6 needles.

SPECIAL ABBREVIATIONS
C4F: Slip next 2 stitches onto cable needle and hold at front, k2 from left-hand needle, k2 from cable needle.

Socks
With US 6 needles cast on 60 stitches.
Distribute stitches evenly onto 3 needles as follows: needle one, 20 stitches; needle two, 20 stitches; needle three, 20 stitches.
(20–20–20 stitches)
RIB PATTERN
Rib round: [K2, p2] twice, *k2, p3, [k2, p2] twice, repeat from * to end.

This round forms the rib pattern.
MAIN PATTERN
Round 1: K2, p1, C4F, p1, [k1, yo, sl1, k1, psso, k1, k2tog, yo, k1, p1, C4F, p1] to end.
Rounds 2 and 4: K2, [p1, k4, p1, k7] to last 6 stitches, p1, k4, p1.
Round 3: K2, p1, k4, p1, [k2, yo, sl1, k2tog, psso, yo, k2, p1, k4, p1] to end.
These 4 rounds form the pattern.
Repeat the last 4 rounds until sock measures 12in from the cast-on edge, ending with either round 2 or 4 of the main pattern.
Work in rib pattern for 4 rounds.
SHAPE HEEL
Rearrange stitches for the heel as follows: needle one, knit 15 stitches; needle three, slip last 15 stitches onto end of first needle.
These 30 stitches are worked to create the heel. Leave the remaining stitches on the two needles for the instep.
Keeping rib pattern correct, continue in rib pattern until 21 rows have been worked, ending with a wrong-side row.
Next row: K19, k2tog, turn.
Next row (wrong side): P10, p2tog, turn.
Next row (right side): K10, k2tog, turn.
Repeat the last 2 rows 4 times more, ending with a right-side row.
Next row (wrong side): P10, p2tog, turn.
(18 stitches)
Next row: K6.
Slip the 30 stitches for instep onto one needle.
Rearrange stitches as follows: needle one, work remaining 9 stitches of heel in pattern,

then pick up and knit 12 stitches along side of heel; needle two, work main pattern across 30 instep stitches; needle three, pick up and knit 12 stitches along other side of heel and remaining 9 stitches of heel.
(21–30–21 stitches)

SHAPE INSTEP

Next round: Work in pattern.

Next round: Needle one, work in pattern to last 3 stitches, k2tog, k1; needle two, work in pattern; needle 3, k1, k2togtbl, work in pattern to end of needle.

Repeat the last 2 rounds until 60 stitches remain. *(15–30–15 stitches)*

Continue without shaping in rib pattern until foot measures 6¼in (or desired length) from the start of heel shaping.

SHAPE TOE

Next round: Needle one, work in pattern to last 3 stitches, k2tog, k1; needle two, k1, k2togtbl, work in pattern to last 3 stitches on second needle, k2tog, k1; needle three, k1, k2togtbl, work in pattern to end of needle.

Repeat this round until 20 stitches remain. *(5–10–5 stitches)*

Work in pattern for 1 round.

Knit 5 stitches from the first needle and slip 5 stitches from the third needle onto end of the first needle.

Kitchener stitch stitches together.

For second sock, repeat from cast on.

Finish

Weave in ends.

SULKA
extra long, chunky scarf

In those cold, winter months it is lovely to wrap up with a long, chunky scarf and the Sulka yarns are such fun to knit with that the knitting of the scarf is just as pleasurable as wearing the scarf.

MEASUREMENTS

9in x 96¼in

MATERIALS

Worsted (CYCA Medium #4) yarn
Mirasol Sulka (60% Merino Wool, 20% Alpaca, 20% Silk; 55yd/50g):
Twelve skeins #213.
(photographed in Marshmallow)

NEEDLES

One pair of US 10 knitting needles
Cable needle
Knitter's sewing needle or tapestry needle

GAUGE

18 stitches and 22 rows to 4in square over pattern using US 10 needles.

SPECIAL ABBREVIATIONS

C4B: Slip next 2 stitches onto cable needle and hold at back, k2 from left-hand needle, k2 from cable needle.
C4F: Slip next 2 stitches onto cable needle and hold at front, k2 from left-hand needle, k2 from cable needle.

Scarf

With US 10 needles, cast on 42 stitches.

RIB PATTERN

Row 1 (right side): P2, [k3, p2] to end.
Row 2: K2, [p3, k2] to end.
Repeat the last 2 rows once more.

CABLE PATTERN

Row 1 (right side): P2, [k4, C4F, p2] to end.
Row 2 and every alternate row: K2, [p8, k2] to end.
Row 3: P2, [k8, p2] to end.
Row 5: Repeat row 1.
Row 7: P2, [C4B, k4, p2] to end.
Row 9: Repeat row 3.
Row 11: Repeat row 7
Row 12: K2, [p8, k2] to end.
These 12 rows form the cable pattern.
Repeat the last 12 rows until the work measures 95½in from the cast-on edge, ending with a wrong-side row.
Starting with row 1 of the rib pattern, work 4 rows in rib.
Bind off.

Finish

Weave in ends.

SULKA
seed stitch, floppy hat

Nothing is as comfy as a warm head and nothing beats the warmth of the Sulka yarn. The floppy nature of the hat means it isn't too tight on your head and it is easy to wear.

MEASUREMENTS
Circumference: 19¾in

MATERIALS
Worsted (CYCA Medium #4) yarn
Mirasol Sulka (60% Merino Wool, 20% Alpaca, 20% Silk; 55yd/50g):
Three skeins #203.
(photographed in Wine)

NEEDLES
One pair of US 8 knitting needles
One pair of US 10 knitting needles
Knitter's sewing needle or tapestry needle

GAUGE
14 stitches and 26 rows to 4in square over seed stitch using US 10 needles.

Hat
With US 8 needles, cast on 70 stitches.
RIB PATTERN
Row 1 (right side): K2, [p2, k2] to end.
Row 2: P2, [k2, p2] to end.
Repeat the last 2 rows once more.
Change to US 10 needles.
MAIN PATTERN
Row 1: [K1, p1] to end.
Row 2: [P1, k1] to end.
These 2 rows form the seed stitch pattern.

Repeat the last 2 rows until hat measures 7¾in from the cast-on edge, ending with a wrong-side row.
SHAPE CROWN
Row 1 (right side): K1, p1, [k2tog, k1, p1] to end. *(53 stitches)*
Row 2: P1, [k2, p1] to last stitch, k1.
Row 3: K1, p1, [k2tog, p1] to end. *(36 stitches)*
Row 4: [P1, k1] to end.
Row 5: [K1, p1, k2tog, k1, p1] to end. *(30 stitches)*
Row 6: [P1, k2, p1, k1] to end.
Row 7: [K1, p1, k2tog, p1] to end. *(24 stitches)*
Row 8: [P1, k1] to end.
Row 9: [K2tog] to end. *(12 stitches)*
Row 10: [P2tog] to end. *(6 stitches)*
Break off yarn. Thread through 6 stitches.
Pull securely and fasten off.

Finish
Sew up back seam.
Weave in ends.

K'ACHA
mock-cable beret

A beret is a classic, a favorite that takes any fashion trend and makes it individual. The mock-cable pattern enhances the decreases around the crown as well as creating an interesting texture to knit.

MEASUREMENTS
Circumference: 19¼in

MATERIALS
DK (CYCA Light #3) yarn
Mirasol K'acha (60% Fine Merino Wool, 25% Alpaca, 15% Silk; 98yd/50g):
Two skeins #1203.
(photographed in Kingfisher Blue)

NEEDLES
One pair of US 6 knitting needles
Cable needle
Knitter's sewing needle or tapestry needle

GAUGE
20 stitches and 26 rows to 4in square over stockinette stitch using US 6 needles.

SPECIAL ABBREVIATIONS
C3B: Slip next 2 stitches onto a cable needle and hold at back of work, knit next stitch from left-hand needle, then knit stitches from cable needle.
C3F: Slip next stitch onto a cable needle and hold at front of work, knit next 2 stitches from left-hand needle, then knit stitch from cable needle.

Hat
With US 6 needles, cast on 98 stitches.
RIB PATTERN
Row 1 (wrong side): K2, [p2, k2] to end.
Row 2: P2, [k2, p2] to end.
Repeat the last 2 rows once more.
CABLE PATTERN
Row 1 (wrong side): K2, [p6, k2] to end.
Row 2: P2, [k2, sl2, k2, p1, m1, p1] to last 8 stitches, k2, sl2, k2, p2. *(109 stitches)*
Row 3: K2, [p2, sl2, p2, k3] to last 8 stitches, p2, sl2, p2, k2.
Row 4: P2, [C3B, C3F, p3] to last 8 stitches, C3B, C3F, p2.
Row 5: K2, [p6, k3] to last 8 stitches, p6, k2.
Row 6: P2, [k2, sl2, k2, p2, m1, p1] to last 8 stitches, k2, sl2, k2, p2. *(120 stitches)*
Row 7: K2, [p2, sl2, p2, k4] to last 8 stitches, p2, sl2, p2, k2.
Row 8: P2, [C3B, C3F, p4] to last 8 stitches, C3B, C3F, p2.
Row 9: K2, [p6, k4] to last 8 stitches, p6, k2.
Row 10: P2, [k2, sl2, k2, p2, m1, p2] to last 8 stitches, k2, sl2, k2, p2.
(131 stitches)
These rows set the position of the increases and cable patterning.
Keeping pattern correct, continue to increase in this way on every following alternate row until there are 186 stitches, ending with a right-side row.
Work 7 rows in pattern.

SHAPE CROWN

Decrease row (right side): P2, [k2, sl2, k2, p2tog, p8] to last 8 stitches, k2, sl2, k2, p2. *(175 stitches)*

This row sets the position of the decrease stitches, continue to decrease in this way on every 4th row until there are 98 stitches. Work 3 rows in pattern.

Next row: P2, [slip next 2 stitches onto a cable needle and hold at back of work, knit next stitch from left hand needle, then k2tog from cable needle, slip next stitch onto a cable needle and hold at front of work, k2tog from left hand needle, then knit stitch from cable needle, p2] to end. *(74 stitches)*

Work 3 rows in pattern.

Next row: P2, [k2tog, sl1, k1, psso, p2] to end. *(50 stitches)*

Work 5 rows in pattern.

Next row: P2tog, [k2tog, p2tog] to end. *(25 stitches)*

Work one row in pattern.

Next row: [K2tog] to last stitch, k1. *(13 stitches)*

Next row: [P2tog] to last stitch, p1. *(7 stitches)*

Break off yarn. Thread through 7 stitches. Pull securely and fasten off.

Finish

Sew back seam together.

Weave in ends.

AKAPANA
mittens with finger-flap

In the cold, winter months warm hands make all the difference, however, when you have to take your mittens off and on your hands can easily get cold. My solution mittens with a flap cover.

SIZE
To fit small to average-sized hand

MATERIALS
Worsted (CYCA Medium #4) yarn
Mirasol Akapana (65% Baby Llama, 25% Merino Wool, 10% Donegal; 95yd/50g): Two skeins #1308.
(photographed in Navy Brights)

NEEDLES
Set of 4 double pointed US 6 knitting needles
Two stitch holders
Knitter's sewing needle or tapestry needle

GAUGE
22 stitches and 26 rows to 4in square over pattern using US 6 needles.

Rib edging (make two)
With US 6 needles, cast on 18 stitches.
RIB PATTERN
Row 1: P2, [k2, p2] to end.
Row 2: K2, [p2, k2] to end.
Repeat the last 2 rows until 8 rows have been worked.
Leave stitches on a stitch holder.

First mitten
With US 6 needles, cast on 36 stitches.
Distribute stitches evenly onto three needles as follows: needle one, 12 stitches; needle two, 12 stitches; needle three, 12 stitches. *(12–12–12 stitches)*
Work in rounds as follows:
Round 1: [K2, p2] to end.
Repeat the last 2 rounds until mitten measures 4¾in from the cast-on edge.
Shape thumb in stockinette stitch as follows:
SHAPE THUMB
Next round: Needle one, k6, m1, k1, m1; needles two and three, knit to end. *(14–12–12 stitches)*
Knit 3 rounds.

121

Next round: Needle one, k6, m1, k3, m1; needles two and three, knit to end. *(16–12–12 stitches)*

Knit 3 rounds.

Next round: Needle one, k6, m1, k5, m1; needles two and three, knit to end. *(18–12–12 stitches)*

Knit one round.

WORK THUMB

Next round: Needle one, k14, turn and slip first 4 stitches onto third needle. Slip remaining 4 stitches on first needle onto second needle.

Working in rows on these 10 stitches only, cast on 2 stitches, knit to end. *(12 stitches)*

Work 7 rows in stockinette stitch.

Next row: [K2tog] to end. *(6 stitches)*

Next row: [P2tog] to end. *(3 stitches)*

Break off yarn. Thread through 3 stitches. Pull securely and fasten off.

WORK HAND

Rearrange the stitches as follows; needle one (one of the two spare needles), slip 4 stitches from needle three (the needle to the right of the thumb), with wrong sides of thumb together, rejoin yarn, with needle one starting from edge, pick up and knit 4 stitches along the cast-on edge of thumb, knit 4 stitches from second needle (needle to the left of the thumb); needle two, knit 12 stitches; needle three, knit 12 stitches.

(12–12–12 stitches)

Next round: Needle one, k6, p2, k2, p2; needle two, [k2, p2] to end; needle three, knit to end.

Repeat the last round 7 times more.

Next round: Needle one, k6, cast (bind) off remaining 6 stitches; needle two, bind off all 12 stitches; needle three, knit to end.

Next round: Needle one, k6, pick up and knit 6 stitches from rib edging on stitch holder; needle two, pick up and knit 12 stitches from rib edging on stitch holder; needle three, knit to end.

Starting with a knit round, continue in stockinette stitch until top measures 2¾in from base of thumb seam.

SHAPE TOP

Next round: Needle one, k4, k2togtbl, k2tog, k4; needle two, knit to last 2 stitches, k2togtbl; needle three, k2tog, knit to end.

Next round: Needle one, k3, k2togtbl, k2tog, k3; needle two, knit to last 2 stitches, k2togtbl; needle three, k2tog, knit to end.

Next round: Needle one, k2, k2togtbl, k2tog, k2; needle two, knit to last 2 stitches, k2togtbl; needle three, k2tog, knit to end.

Next round: Needle one, k1, k2togtbl, k2tog, k1; needle two, knit to last 2 stitches, k2togtbl; needle three, k2tog, knit to end.

Next round: Needle one, k2togtbl, k2tog; needle two, knit to last 2 stitches, k2togtbl; needle three, k2tog, knit to end.

(2–7–7 stitches)

Knit one round.

Slip stitch from first needle onto the third needle then slip remaining stitch on first needle onto second needle.

Kitchener stitch stitches together.

Second mitten

Work as given for first mitten until Work thumb.

Next round: Needle one, k14, turn and slip first 4 of these stitches onto third needle. Slip remaining 4 stitches on first needle onto second needle.

Working in rows on these 10 stitches only, purl 10 stitches, turn and cast on 2 stitches.

(12 stitches)

Work 6 rows in stockinette stitch.

Next row: [K2tog] to end. *(6 stitches)*

Next row: [P2tog] to end. *(3 stitches)*

Break off yarn. Thread through 3 stitches. Pull securely and fasten off.

WORK HAND

Rearrange the stitches as follows; needle one (one of the two spare needles), slip 4 stitches from needle three (the needle to the right of the thumb), with wrong sides of thumb together, rejoin yarn, with needle one starting from edge, pick up and knit 4 stitches along the cast-on edge of thumb, knit 4 stitches from second needle (needle to the left of the thumb); needle two, knit 12 stitches; needle three, knit 12 stitches.

(12–12–12 stitches)

Next round: Needle one, p2, k2, p2, k6 on first needle; needle two, knit to end; needle three, [k2, p2] to end. Repeat the last round 7 times more.

Next round: Needle one, p2, k2, p2, k6; needle two, knit to end; needle three, bind off 12 stitches.

Next round: Needle one, bind off 6 stitches, knit to end; needle two, knit to end; needle three, pick up and knit 12 stitches from rib edging on stitch holder.

Next round: Needle one, pick up and knit remaining 6 stitches from rib edging on stitch holder, k6; needle two, knit to end; needle three, knit to end.

Starting with a knit round, continue in stockinette stitch until top measures 2¾in from base of thumb seam.

Complete as given for first mitten from Shape top.

Finish

Join thumb seams.

Weave in ends.

K'ACHA
fingerless gloves

These fingerless gloves are a joy to wear and the stitch pattern is simply the reverse side of single-row stripes, worked in three shades, in stockinette stitch.

SIZE
To fit small to average-sized hand

MATERIALS
DK (CYCA Light #3) yarn
Mirasol K'acha (60% Fine Merino Wool, 25% Alpaca, 15% Silk; 98yd/50g):
yarn A, one skein #1206;
yarn B, one skein #1203;
yarn C, one skein #1205.
(photographed in: yarn A, Deep Navy; yarn B, Kingfisher Blue; yarn C, Dark Chocolate)

NEEDLES
Set of 4 double pointed US 6 knitting needles
Knitter's sewing needle or tapestry needle

GAUGE
20 stitches and 30 rows to 4in square over pattern using US 6 needles.

First mitten
With US 6 needles and yarn A, cast on 36 stitches. Distribute stitches evenly onto 3 needles as follows: needle one, 12 stitches; needle two, 12 stitches; needle three, 12 stitches. *(12–12–12 stitches)*
Work in rounds as follows:

STRIPE PATTERN
Round 1 (wrong side): With yarn B, knit.
Round 2: With yarn C, knit to end.
Round 3: With yarn A, knit to end.

These 3 rounds form the 3 stripe pattern. Repeat throughout.
Continue in stripe pattern until work measures 4¾in from the cast-on edge.

SHAPE THUMB
Next round: Needle one, k6, m1, k1, m1; needles two and three, knit to end. *(14–12–12 stitches)*
Knit 3 rounds.
Next round: Needle one, k6, m1, k3, m1; needles two and three, knit to end. *(16–12–12 stitches)*
Knit 3 rounds.
Next round: Needle one, k6, m1, k5, m1; needles two and three, knit to end. *(18–12–12 stitches)*
Knit one round.

WORK THUMB
Next round: Needle one, k14, turn and slip first 4 of these stitches onto third needle. Slip remaining 4 stitches on first needle onto second needle.
Working in rows on these 10 stitches only, cast on 3 stitches. *(13 stitches)*
Work 8 rows in stripe pattern.
Bind off.

WORK HAND
Working in the stripe pattern, rearrange the stitches as follows; needle one (one of the two spare needles), slip 4 stitches from needle three (the needle to the right of the thumb), with wrong sides of thumb together, rejoin yarn, with needle one starting from

124

edge, pick up and knit 4 stitches along the cast-on edge of thumb, knit 4 stitches from second needle (needle to the left of the thumb); needle two, knit 12 stitches; needle three, knit 12 stitches. *(12–12–12 stitches)* Continue in pattern until top measures 2in. Bind off.

Second mitten
Work as given for first mitten until Work thumb.

WORK THUMB
Next round: Needles one and two, knit to end; needle three, k14, turn and slip first 4 stitches of third needle onto second needle. Slip remaining 4 stitches on third needle onto first needle.
Working in rows on these 10 stitches only, cast on 3 stitches. *(13 stitches)*
Work 8 rows in stripe pattern.
Bind off.

WORK HAND
Working in the stripe pattern, rearrange the stitches as follows; needle three (one of the two spare needles), slip last 4 stitches from needle two (the needle to the right of the thumb), with wrong sides of thumb together, rejoin yarn, with needle three, starting from edge, pick up and knit 4 stitches along the cast-on edge of thumb, then, knit 4 stitches from first needle (the needle to the left of the thumb); needle two, knit 12 stitches; needle one, knit 12 stitches. *(12–12–12 stitches)* Continue in pattern until top measures 2in. Bind off.

Finish
Join thumb seams.
Weave in ends.

HACHO
lace, skinny scarf

This beautiful skinny scarf is the perfect accessory for both casual and more formal outfits and is an easy weekend project to knit. Add beads or sequins to your scarf for a little sparkle.

MEASUREMENTS
2½in x 78¾in approx.

MATERIALS
DK (CYCA Light #3) yarn
Mirasol Hacho (100% Wool; 137yd/50g):
Two skeins #304.
(photographed in Hacho, Sapphire Jade)
For a single shade alternative: Mirasol Tupa,
(50% Merino Wool, 50% Silk; 137yd/50g)

NEEDLES
One pair of US 6 knitting needles.
Knitter's sewing needle or tapestry needle

GAUGE
10 stitches to 2½in and 34 rows to 4in square over pattern using US 6 needles.

Scarf
With US 6 needles, cast on 10 stitches.
Knit one row.
MAIN PATTTERN
Row 1: Sl1, k1, [yo, k2tog] twice, [yo] 4 times, k2tog, yo, p2tog.
Row 2: Yo, p2tog, k1, [k1, p1] twice into the large yo loop, [k1, p1] twice, k2.
Row 3: Sl1, [k1, yo, k2tog] twice, k4, yo, p2tog.
Row 4: Yo, p2tog, k5, [p1, k2] twice.
Row 5: Sl1, k1, yo, k2tog, k2, yo, k2tog, k3, yo, p2tog.

Row 6: Yo, p2tog, k4, p1, k3, p1, k2.
Row 7: Sl1, k1, yo, k2tog, k3, yo, k2tog, k2, yo, p2tog.
Row 8: Yo, p2tog, k3, p1, k4, p1, k2.
Row 9: Sl1, k1, yo, k2tog, k4, yo, k2tog, k1, yo, p2tog.
Row 10: Yo, p2tog, k2, p1, k5, p1, k2.
Row 11: Sl1, k1, yo, k2tog, k5, yo, k2tog, yo, p2tog.
Row 12: Bind off 3 stitches, then slip the stitch from right-hand needle back onto the left-hand needle, yo, p2tog, k5, p1, k2.
These 12 rows form the pattern.
Repeat the last 12 rows until scarf measures 78¾in from the cast-on edge, (or keep knitting until both hanks are used up) ending with row 12 of the pattern.
Knit one row.
Bind off.

Finish
Weave in ends.

distributors

USA
Knitting Fever Inc
315 Bayview Ave,
Amityville,
New York11701
Tel: (+516) 546 3600
Fax: (+516) 546 6871
www.knittingfever.com

CANADA
Diamond Yarn Ltd
155 Martin Ross Avenue,
Unit 3, Toronto,
Ontario. M3J 2L9
Tel: (+416) 736 6111
Fax: (+416) 736 6112
www.diamondyarn.com

NORWAY
Du Store Alpakka AS
Mohagasvingen 4,
2770, Jaren.
Tel: (+47) 61 32 70 90
www.dustorealpakka.com

SPAIN/FRANCE/GERMANY/
LUXEMBOURG/BELGIUM/
HOLLAND
Katia
Av. Catalunya, s/n-08296,
Castellbell I el Vilar (Barcelona).
Tel: (+34) 93 834 02 01
www.katia.es
France
Tel: (+34) 93 834 10 88

GERMANY
Designer Yarns (Deutschland) GmbH
Sachsstrasse 30,
D-50259, Pulheim Brauweiler
Tel: (+49) 2234 205453
Fax: (+49) 2234 205456
www.designeryarns.de

UNITED KINGDOM
Designer Yarns Ltd
Units 8-10 Newbridge Industrial Estate,
Pitt Street,
Keighley,
West Yorkshire
BD21 4PQ
Tel: (+44) 01535 664222
Fax: (+44) 01535 664333
Email: alex@designeryarns.uk.com
www.designeryarns.uk.com

Websites
The Mirasol Yarn Collection website:
www.mirasolperu.com

Jane Ellison's website:
www.janeellison.co.uk

acknowledgements

There are many talented and gifted people who have lent their skills to the production of this book. Getting a knitting book together is never easy and has lots and lots of intricate details that need dedication and, most importantly, a love of your work to complete. Thank you to all of you who have worked so hard, especially Luise, to get this book together and made it fun to work on.

I am grateful to Sion Elalouf from Knitting Fever for asking me to design and be so involved with the Mirasol Yarn Collection and recognizing that this would be something very close to my heart. A special thank you also to Peter Mulley from Diamond Yarn and Raul Rivera from Michell for all their support. And, a special acknowledgement to Kari Hestnes who, to me, is the mother of the Mirasol Project.

Thank you to my knitters who constantly produce hand knits to a fantastic standard within very tight deadlines. Your talents and commitment to making high quality garments is amazing.

credits

The publisher would like thank pattern checker Sue Whiting, Luise Roberts for her excellent editorial and design input, and models Joanna Heygate, Luisa Savoia and Melissa Spencer.